Investigation of the Potential Source Area, Contamination Pathway, and Probable Release History of Chlorinated-Solvent-Contaminated Groundwater at the Capital City Plume Site, Montgomery, Alabama, 2008–2010

By James E. Landmeyer, Scott Miller, Bruce G. Campbell, Don A. Vroblesky, Amy C. Gill, and Athena P. Clark

Prepared in cooperation with the U.S. Environmental Protection Agency, Region 4, Superfund Division, Superfund Remedial Branch, Section C

Scientific Investigations Report 2011–5148

U.S. Department of the Interior
U.S. Geological Survey

U.S. Department of the Interior
KEN SALAZAR, Secretary

U.S. Geological Survey
Marcia K. McNutt, Director

U.S. Geological Survey, Reston, Virginia: 2011

For more information on the USGS—the Federal source for science about the Earth, its natural and living resources, natural hazards, and the environment, visit *http://www.usgs.gov* or call 1-888-ASK-USGS

For an overview of USGS information products, including maps, imagery, and publications, visit *http://www.usgs.gov/pubprod*

To order this and other USGS information products, visit *http://store.usgs.gov*

Suggested citation:
Landmeyer, J.E., Miller, S., Campbell, B.G., Vroblesky, D.A., Gill, A.C., and Clark, A.P., 2011, Investigation of the potential source area, contamination pathway, and probable release history of chlorinated-solvent-contaminated groundwater at the Capital City Plume Site, Montgomery, Alabama, 2008–2010: U.S. Geological Survey Scientific Investigations Report 2011–5148, 53 p.

Contents

Figures

Tables

Acknowledgments

The authors thank Rusty Kestle, U.S. Environmental Protection Agency, formerly of the Alabama Department of Environmental Management, who assisted with field work at the Capital City Plume Site during August 2008 and who, in 1993, correctly commented that additional groundwater sampling would be necessary to fully understand the extent and history of the groundwater contamination at the Capital City Plume Site. The authors thank Thomas R. "Buddy" Morgan, General Manager, Montgomery Water Works and Sanitary Sewer Board for his insight on the history of the sanitary sewer and stormwater systems in downtown Montgomery. The authors appreciate the assistance of the late Kenneth J. Groves, Jr., former Director, Planning and Development, and thank Russell Stringer, Urban Forester, both with the City of Montgomery.

The authors thank L. Elliott Jones, Will S. Mooty, and Richard S. Moreland of the U.S. Geological Survey for their help with field work during 2008–2010. The authors thank John G. Schumacher and Matthew D. Petkewich of the U.S. Geological Survey for their thorough review of this report.

Finally, we thank the citizens of Montgomery for their interest and hospitality during our field work in Montgomery.

Conversion Factors and Datums

Multiply	By	To obtain
Length		
inch	2.54	centimeter (cm)
inch	25.4	millimeter (mm)
foot (ft)	0.3048	meter (m)
mile (mi)	1.609	kilometer (km)
Flow rate		
foot per year (ft/yr)	0.3048	meter per year (m/yr)
inch per year (in/yr)	25.4	millimeter per year (mm/yr)

Temperature in degrees Celsius (°C) may be converted to degrees Fahrenheit (°F) as follows:

$$°F = (1.8 \times °C) + 32$$

Temperature in degrees Fahrenheit (°F) may be converted to degrees Celsius (°C) as follows:

$$°C = (°F - 32) / 1.8$$

Vertical coordinate information is referenced to the National Geodetic Vertical Datum of 1929 (NGVD 29).

Altitude, as used in this report, refers to distance above the vertical datum.

Specific conductance is given in microsiemens per centimeter at 25 degrees Celsius (µS/cm at 25 °C).

Concentrations of chemical constituents in water are given either in milligrams per liter (mg/L), micrograms per liter (µg/L), picograms per kilogram (pg/kg; where 1 pg/kg is equivalent to 1.0×10^{-9} mg/L), or moles per kilogram (Mol/kg).

Concentrations of chemical constituents in tree cores are given in milligrams per kilogram (mg/kg).

Headspace volume is given in cubic centimeters (cm^3).

Acronyms and Abbreviations Used in This Report

<	less than
>	greater than
ADEM	Alabama Department of Environmental Management
BTEX	benzene, toluene, ethylbenzene, and xylenes
CCP	Capital City Plume
CERCLA	Comprehensive Environmental Response, Compensation, and Liability Act
CFC	chlorofluorocarbon
CFC-11	trichlorofluoromethane
CFC-113	1,1,2-trichloro-1,2,2-trifluoroethane
cis-1,2-DCE	*cis*-1,2-dichloroethylene
Cl:Na	chloride to sodium ratio
CCl_4	carbon tetrachloride
1,1-DCE	1,1-dichloroethylene
DO	dissolved oxygen
E	estimated concentration
ESA	environmental site assessment
FID	flame-ionization detector
GC/PID	gas chromatography/photoionization detection
MCL	maximum contaminant level
MDL	method detection level
mg/kg	milligrams per kilogram
MRL	method reporting level
MTBE	methyl *tert*-butyl ether
MWWSSB	Montgomery Water Works and Sanitary Sewer Board
NPDWR	National Primary Drinking Water Regulations
NPL	National Priorities List
NSDWR	National Secondary Drinking Water Regulations
NTU	nephelometric turbidity units
NWQL	National Water Quality Laboratory (U.S. Geological Survey)
PCE	perchloroethylene
PDB	passive diffusion bag
pg/kg	picogram per kilogram
PID	photo-ionization detector
PIXE	proton-induced x-ray emission
ppbv	parts per billion by volume
ppm	parts per million
RI	remedial investigation
RSA	Retirement Systems of Alabama
SC	specific conductance
SF_6	sulfur hexafluoride
1,1,1-TCA	1,1,1-trichloroethane
TCE	trichloroethylene
USEPA	U.S. Environmental Protection Agency
USGS	U.S. Geological Survey
VOA	volatile organic analysis
VOC	volatile organic compounds

Investigation of the Potential Source Area, Contamination Pathway, and Probable Release History of Chlorinated-Solvent-Contaminated Groundwater at the Capital City Plume Site, Montgomery, Alabama, 2008–2010

By James E. Landmeyer,[1] Scott Miller,[2] Bruce G. Campbell,[1] Don A. Vroblesky,[1] Amy C. Gill,[3] and Athena P. Clark[3]

Abstract

Detection of the organic solvent perchloroethylene (PCE) in a shallow public-supply well in 1991 and exposure of workers in 1993 to solvent vapors during excavation activities to depths near the water table provided evidence that the shallow aquifer beneath the capital city of Montgomery, Alabama, was contaminated. Investigations conducted from 1993 to 1999 by State and Federal agencies confirmed the detection of PCE in the shallow aquifer, as well as the detection of the organic solvent trichloroethylene (TCE) and various inorganic compounds, but the source of the groundwater contamination was not determined. In May 2000 the U.S. Environmental Protection Agency proposed that the site, called the Capital City Plume (CCP) Site, be a candidate for the National Priorities List. Between 2000 and 2007, numerous site-investigation activities also did not determine the source of the groundwater contamination.

In 2008, additional assessments were conducted at the CCP Site to investigate the potential source area, contamination pathway, and the probable release history of the chlorinated-solvent-contaminated groundwater. The assessments included the collection of (1) pore water in 2008 from the hyporheic zone of a creek using passive-diffusion bag samplers; (2) tissue samples in 2008 and 2009 from trees growing in areas of downtown Montgomery characterized by groundwater contamination and from trees growing in riparian zones along the Alabama River and Cypress Creek; and (3) groundwater samples in 2009 and 2010. The data collected were used to investigate the potential source area of contaminants detected in groundwater, the pathway of groundwater contamination, and constraints on the probable contaminant-release history.

[1]U.S. Geological Survey, Columbia, South Carolina.

[2]U.S. Environmental Protection Agency, Region 4, Atlanta, Georgia.

[3]U.S. Geological Survey, Montgomery, Alabama.

The data collected between 2008 and 2010 indicate that the PCE and TCE contamination of the shallow aquifer beneath the CCP Site most likely resulted from the past use and disposal of industrial wastewater from printing operations containing chlorinated solvents into the sanitary sewer and (or) stormwater systems of Montgomery. Moreover, chlorinated-solvent use and disposal occurred at least between the 1940s and 1970s at several locations occupied by printing operations. The data also indicate that PCE and TCE contamination continues to occur in the shallow subsurface near potential release areas and that PCE and TCE have been transported to the intermediate part of the shallow aquifer.

Introduction

The Capital City Plume (CCP) Site is characterized by shallow groundwater contamination beneath a widespread area of downtown Montgomery, Alabama. The primary contaminant is perchloroethylene (PCE), but other volatile organic compounds (VOCs), such as trichloroethylene (TCE), and inorganic compounds, such as chromium, have been detected (Black & Veatch, 2002; Malcolm Pirnie, Inc., 2003; Alabama Department of Public Health, 2004; Hall, 2007). PCE is of concern because it was detected in a Montgomery public-supply well in 1991 at concentrations of 7.1 micrograms per liter (μg/L) and at 160 μg/L in 2009—both above the U.S. Environmental Protection Agency (USEPA; 2009b) National Primary Drinking Water Regulations (NPDWR) maximum contaminant level (MCL) of 5 μg/L (*http://water.epa.gov/drink/contaminants/index.cfm*, accessed March 3, 2011).

Although PCE was synthesized as early as 1821, widespread usage to meet industrial needs for an effective solvent with decreased flammability did not start until after the 1940s (U.S. Environmental Protection Agency, 2000a). PCE can cause various human health problems ranging from dizziness and headaches to death (Alabama Department of Public Health, 2004). The organic solvent TCE was synthesized in the 1920s and also is used as a non-flammable solvent. Chromium is the primary inorganic compound of concern in groundwater at the CCP Site (Black & Veatch, 2002; Malcolm Pirnie, Inc., 2003; Alabama Department of Public Health, 2004; Hall, 2007) and although present in some groundwater samples, chromium has not been detected in any of the public-supply wells at the site in concentrations greater than the NPDWR MCL of 100 µg/L (U.S. Environmental Protection Agency, 2009b).

Previous investigations between 1991 and 2008 to delineate the groundwater contamination at the CCP Site did not identify the source of the contamination. In 2008, the U.S. Geological Survey (USGS) Alabama and South Carolina Water Science Centers, in cooperation with the USEPA, Region 4, Superfund Division, Superfund Remedial Branch, Section C, conducted additional assessments to investigate the potential source area, contamination pathway, and the probable release history of the organic contaminants in groundwater at the CCP Site. These assessments included the following:

1. The collection of pore-water samples during August 2008, using passive-diffusion bag (PDB) samplers in the hyporheic zone of Cypress Creek, a tributary to the Alabama River downgradient from the CCP Site;

2. The collection of tissue samples during August 2008 and January 2009 from trees growing in downtown Montgomery in areas characterized by groundwater contamination and samples from trees in the riparian zones along the Alabama River and Cypress Creek; and

3. The collection of groundwater samples during April–May 2009 and during May 2010.

Purpose and Scope

This report describes additional assessment activities conducted during 2008–2010 to investigate the potential source area, contamination pathway, and probable release history of chlorinated-solvent-contaminated groundwater at the CCP Site in downtown Montgomery, Alabama. The scope of these additional assessments included the installation during August 2008 and analysis of three PDB samplers in the hypo-rheic zone of Cypress Creek and the collection and analysis of cores collected from 69 trees growing in and around downtown Montgomery; the collection and analysis during April–May 2009 of water samples from 13 monitoring wells in downtown Montgomery and collection and analysis during May 2010 of groundwater samples for age date determination.

Description of Study Area

The City of Montgomery is located in the northern part of the Eastern Gulf Section of the Coastal Plain Physiographic Province (fig. 1). The city, which was incorporated on December 3, 1819, is located on a bluff near a sharp meander of the Alabama River. The bluff is composed of, in ascending order, Cretaceous and Quaternary sand, gravel, silt, and clay up to 260 feet (ft) above the current stream-bed altitude of the Alabama River, and was created during the Quaternary period by the downcutting ancestral Alabama River as it adjusted to lower sea levels (Robinson, 2002).

The geologic units beneath the City of Montgomery include in ascending order pre-Cretaceous crystalline rock overlain by sediments of Cretaceous age overlain by surficial sediments of Quaternary age (fig. 2; Knowles and others, 1963; Robinson, 2002). Pre-Cretaceous schist and gneiss are overlain unconformably by the Coker Formation. The top of the Coker Formation is about 500 to 700 ft below land surface in the study area (Knowles and others, 1963). The Gordo Formation unconformably overlies the Coker Formation. The Eutaw Formation rests unconformably on the Gordo Forma-tion of the Tuscaloosa Group. Although part of the Eutaw Formation is exposed in downtown Montgomery, most of the Eutaw Formation in the study area is covered by Quaternary alluvial and terrace deposits. Cretaceous sediments of the Eutaw Formation can be found at depths between 0 and 400 ft below land surface. The Quaternary sediments include alluvial and terrace deposits of sand, gravel, silt, and clay to depths between 0 and 100 ft below land surface in some parts of the CCP Site study area.

The alluvial and terrace deposits of Quaternary age yield water to wells screened to depths between 50 and 100 ft below land surface. These deposits collectively form the shallow part of the shallow aquifer beneath Montgomery (fig. 2), and wells screened across these depths have similar water-level altitudes (Scott and others, 1987; Robinson, 2002). Wells screened in the shallow aquifer are used for public supply in Montgomery (wells 9W and 9E; fig. 3). In general, the depth to the water table in the shallow aquifer ranges from about 35 to 55 ft below land surface in downtown Montgomery, depending on the location. Most of the shallow monitoring wells installed during previous investigations to define the generalized boundary of the CCP Site are screened in the shallow-aquifer sediments (wells identified with the suffix S in fig. 3; Black & Veatch, 2002). Some monitoring wells on the CCP Site, however, are screened at depths between 150 and 240 ft below land surface. Previous reports describe these wells as being open to the intermediate part of the shallow aquifer (fig. 2; Black & Veatch, 2002), and this terminology is used in this report (wells identified with the suffix I in fig. 3). The Coker Formation also yields water to municipal wells in Montgomery, but wells drilled to the Coker Formation also are screened in the shallower Gordo and Eutaw Formations; Knowles and others (1963) refer to these sediments as the deep aquifer. The crystalline rocks are considered relatively impermeable and are not used for municipal water supply in the CCP Site area.

The shallow aquifer and the deep aquifer have been used since the 1880s by the City of Montgomery for water supply. Groundwater from these aquifers was the sole source of potable water for Montgomery for at least 100 years (yr).

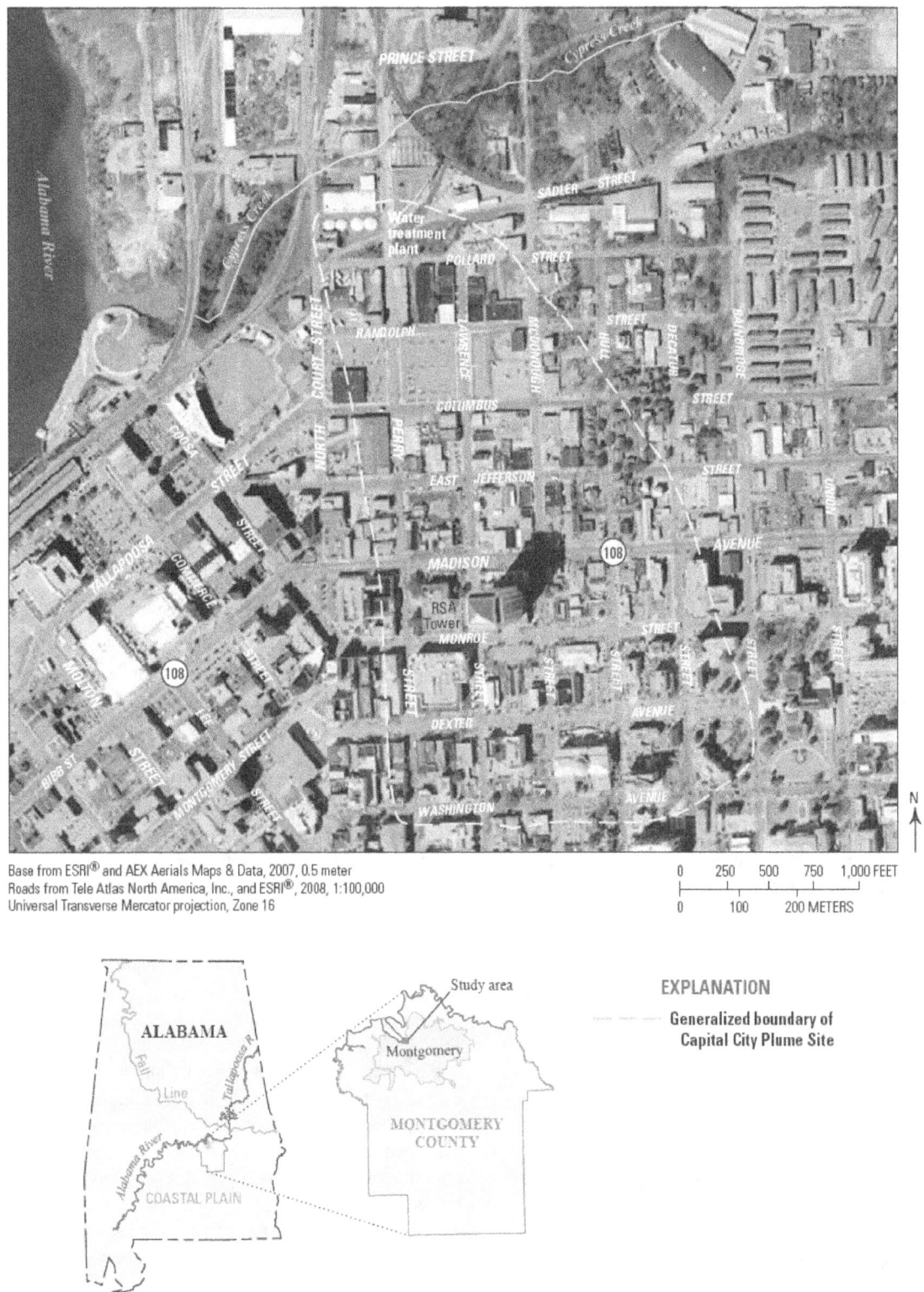

Base from ESRI® and AEX Aerials Maps & Data, 2007, 0.5 meter
Roads from Tele Atlas North America, Inc., and ESRI®, 2008, 1:100,000
Universal Transverse Mercator projection, Zone 16

0   250   500   750   1,000 FEET

0   100   200 METERS

EXPLANATION

Generalized boundary of
Capital City Plume Site

Figure 1. Location of study area and the approximate extent of the Capital City Plume Site, City of Montgomery,
to   Con A b

Period	Stratigraphic unit		Major lithology	Thickness (feet)	Hydrogeologic unit	Regional aquifer system
Quaternary	Alluvial and terrace deposits		Sand, gravel, silt, and clay	30 to 100+	Shallow aquifer, composed of shallow and intermediate aquifers	Southeastern Coastal Plain aquifer system
Cretaceous	Eutaw Formation		Upper and lower marine sand separated by clay; consists of glauconitic sand interbedded with calcareous sandstone and sandy limestone	0 to 400+	Confining unit	
	Tuscaloosa Group	Gordo Formation	Basal zone of gravel and sand overlain by lenticular beds of sand and clay	300+	Gordo aquifer	
					Confining unit	
		Coker Formation	Basal zone of non-marine sand, gravel, and clay; upper zone of marine sand and clay	500+	Coker aquifer	
Pre-Cretaceous			Schist, gneiss	1,000+	Base of freshwater flow system	

Figure 2. Generalized stratigraphic and hydrogeologic units underlying Montgomery, Alabama, and the Capital City Plume Site (modified from Robinson, 2002).

During the 1980s, surface-water resources began to be used and the wells supplied no more than 34 percent of the city's demands. Since about 1997, the Montgomery Water Works and Sanitary Sewer Board (MWWSSB) has relied almost exclusively on the Tallapoosa River for water supply with supplemental supplies derived from groundwater during periods of peak demand and droughts.

Recharge to the shallow aquifer in the study area occurs from precipitation, which averages about 55 inches per year (in/yr; Robinson, 2002). Groundwater in the shallow aquifer flows north-northwest toward the Alabama River (fig. 3; Hall, 2007). Previous investigators determined that the Alabama River flood plain, including Montgomery, is susceptible to contamination from the surface (Scott and others, 1987).

Previous Investigations

Multiple investigations have been performed at the CCP Site since 1991 (table 1). These initial investigations helped to delineate the extent of groundwater contamination. Because some data obtained during previous investigations are used to support conclusions made from data collected during the additional assessments conducted by the USEPA and USGS during 2008–2010, a brief review is warranted.

During April 1991, the MWWSSB sampled public-supply wells in Montgomery pursuant to the USEPA's Wellhead Protection Program (Black & Veatch, 2002). A sample from public-supply well 9 West (9W, fig. 4) contained 7.1 µg/L of PCE, which exceeded the NPDWR MCL of 5 µg/L. Well 9W

is screened from 69 to 79 ft below land surface in the shallow aquifer and had been in use since 1962. Well 9W was shut down in 1992 as a result of the PCE detection. During May 1992, samples from wells 9W and 9 East (9E, fig. 4) both contained 21 µg/L of PCE. Well 9E is screened from 64 to 74 ft below land surface in the shallow aquifer and also was drilled in 1962. Well 9E was shut down in 1997 because of structural problems and PCE detection.

In September 1993, workers were excavating soil from about 25 ft below land surface (slightly above the average depth to water table at that time) to construct the Retirement Systems of Alabama (RSA) Energy Plant at the intersection of Monroe and McDonough Streets (fig. 4). The workers were overcome by acute exposure to vapors later determined to be PCE and possibly TCE (Black & Veatch, 2002). The excavation site is located about 2,280 ft south and upgradient from PCE-contaminated public-supply wells 9W and 9E. In response to this acute exposure, the Alabama Department of Environmental Management (ADEM) conducted Phase I and Phase II investigations at the excavation site in October and November 1993, respectively. During Phase I, soil samples were collected in the RSA Energy Plant area and groundwater samples were collected from shallow monitoring well MW-1S near the excavation; MW-1S contained 607 µg/L PCE. During Phase II, three additional monitoring wells (MW-2S, MW-3S, and MW-4S) were installed in the vicinity of the excavation area near the RSA Energy Plant, and soil-gas samples were collected and analyzed using the PETREX™ tube method (Black & Veatch, 2002). Between 1993 and 1994, PCE- and TCE-contaminated

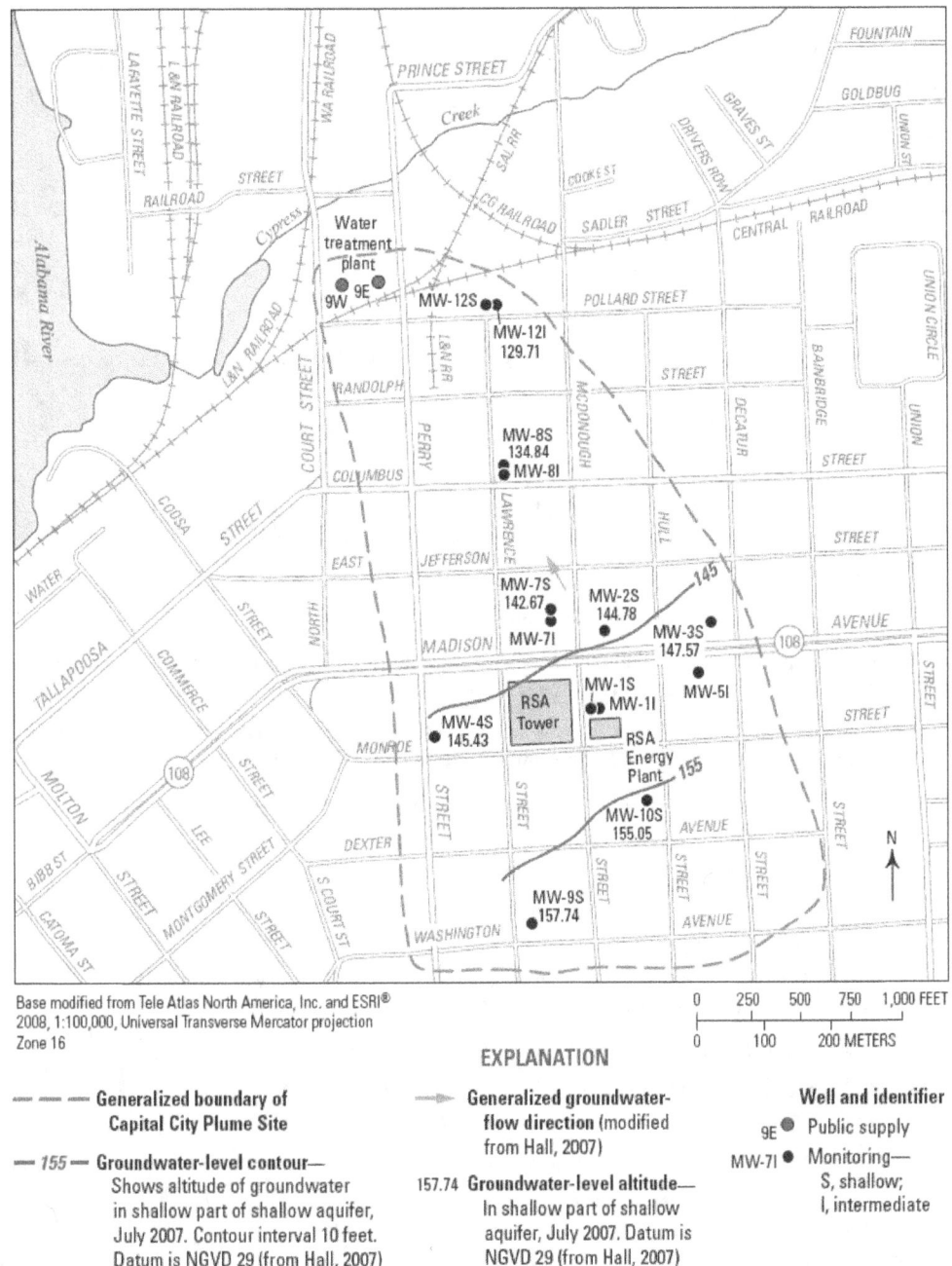

Figure 3. Locations of public-supply and shallow and intermediate monitoring wells, groundwater-level altitudes and generalized groundwater-flow direction in July 2007, and generalized extent of the Capital City Plume Site, Montgomery, Alabama.

soil was identified, removed, and disposed of. During the Phase I and Phase II investigations, no obvious source of the PCE or TCE was observed (Black & Veatch, 2002).

In February 1995, ADEM initiated a Preliminary Assessment in accordance with the Comprehensive Environmental Response, Compensation, and Liability Act (CERCLA), or Superfund, regulations enacted in 1980 (Black & Veatch, 2002). Samples from several temporary monitoring wells that were installed confirmed that PCE and TCE were present in deep

soil and groundwater in parts of downtown Montgomery near the RSA Energy Plant (Black & Veatch, 2002). In 1996, the RSA Tower was built west of and adjacent to the RSA Energy Plant site (fig. 4). At that time, ADEM recommended that the CCP Site be considered for the National Priorities List (NPL).

In 2000, the USEPA proposed to list the CCP Site on the NPL (Federal Register, May 11, 2000) because public-supply wells contained concentrations of PCE greater than the MCL and because the source area, contamination pathway,

Table 1.   Timeline of previous investigations and events important to the additional assessments of the Capital City Plume Site, Montgomery, Alabama, 1819–2010.

[CPI, commercial pringing industry; MWWSSB, Montgomery Water Works and Sanitary Sewer Board; PCE, perchloroethylene; TCE, trichloroethylene; RSA, Retirement Systems of Alabama; ADEM, Alabama Department of Environmental Management; USEPA, U.S. Environmental Protection Agency; NPL, National Priorities List; USGS, U.S. Geological Survey]

Date	Event
1819	The City of Montgomery was incorporated.
1828–29	A CPI was founded in Montgomery.
1850	A CPI was located on Commerce Street.[a]
1855	Building constructed at the southeastern intersection of Dexter Avenue and Lawrence Street occupied by a CPI.
1860s	Montgomery stormwater and sewer systems were built.[b]
1885	Montgomery municipal water is supplied by well fields.[b,c]
1940–41	A CPI relocates from the southeastern intersection of Dexter Avenue and Lawrence Street to the southeastern intersection of Washington Avenue and Lawrence Street, the former location of a competing CPI. The building contained a press room and an 8-unit Goss Headliner letter press. Zinc plates were made on-site.
1941	Well field for City of Montgomery developed.
1950	The MWWSSB took over Montgomery well fields.[c]
1960s	The CPI switches from flammable alcohol-based solvents to nonflammable chlorinated solvents, such as PCE and TCE, to accelerate drying times in the pressroom.
1962–63	The public-supply wells 9W and 9E are drilled in the shallow aquifer and screened from 69 to 79 feet below land surface and from 64 to 74 feet below land surface, respectively.[d,e] A CPI is located on the southeastern intersection of Dexter Avenue and Decatur Street until 1979.
1965	The C.T. Perry Water Purification Plant was built on the Tallapoosa River to treat surface water for municipal distribution. Water was disinfected by chlorination.
1970	Montgomery sewage, previously discharged to the Alabama River, was sent to Econchate wastewater treatment plant.
1970s	A CPI made aluminum plates on-site at the southeastern intersection of Washington Avenue and Lawrence Street. A commercial company laundered soiled rags for the CPI off-site.
1976	Congress enacted the Resource Conservation and Recovery Act (RCRA).
1977	A CPI operated a 9-unit lithographic offset press at the southeastern intersection of Washington Avenue and Lawrence Street that used an ink and water mixture.
1979	A CPI located on the southeastern intersection of Dexter Avenue and Decatur Street discontinues printing.
1980	The Comprehensive Environmental Response, Compensation, and Liability Act (CERCLA), or Superfund, was enacted.
1991–92	PCE was detected in public-supply well 9W in April 1991 at a concentration of 7.1 µg/L and at 21 µg/L in wells 9W and 9E in May 1992; both wells are in the upper part of the shallow aquifer; detections were reported by the MWWSSB.[d]
1992	Well 9W was taken out of service because of PCE contamination.
September 1993	Workers were overcome at about 25 feet below land surface by vapors during soil excavation for the RSA Energy Plant at the northeastern intersection of Monroe Street and McDonough Street. Contaminated soil was excavated and removed.[d]
October 1993	ADEM Phase I Investigation.[d]
November 1993	ADEM Phase II Investigation.[d]
February 1995	The ADEM preliminary assessment confirms detection of PCE in shallow groundwater near the RSA Energy Plant.[d]

Table 1.   Timeline of previous investigations and events important to the additional assessments of the Capital City Plume Site, Montgomery, Alabama, 1819–2010.—Continued

[CPI, commercial pringing industry; MWWSSB, Montgomery Water Works and Sanitary Sewer Board; PCE, perchloroethylene; TCE, trichloroethylene; RSA, Retirement Systems of Alabama; ADEM, Alabama Department of Environmental Management; USEPA, U.S. Environmental Protection Agency; NPL, National Priorities List; USGS, U.S. Geological Survey]

Date	Event
1996	The RSA Tower is built between the intersection of Monroe Street, McDonough Street, Lawrence Street, and Madison Avenue, near the RSA Energy Plant.
	ADEM recommends that the CCP Site be considered for the Superfund list.
1997	Well 9E was taken out of service because of PCE detections.[d]
	A CPI ceases printing operations at the southeastern intersection of Washington Avenue and Lawrence Street.
2000	The USEPA proposes to list the CCP Site on the NPL.
	The USEPA begins a remedial investigation (RI).[b]
2001	The USEPA collects additional soil samples at the RSA Energy Plant.
2002	PCE is detected in Cypress Creek during USEPA sampling.
	City of Montgomery begins Feasibility Study.[f]
	A CPI relocates from the southeastern intersection of Washington Avenue and Lawrence Street to a location on Moulton Street.
2003	The Montgomery County Commission initiates an Environmental Site Assessment of a piece of property once occupied by a CPI at the southeastern intersection of Washington Avenue and Lawrence Street. A CPI that used various offset printing presses ceased operation at the intersection of Washington Avenue and McDonough Street.
2007	The City of Montgomery initiates a groundwater sampling event. Results indicate continued detections of PCE in wells.[g]
August 2008	The USEPA and USGS conduct an assessment of the potential source of groundwater contamination.[h]
January 2009	The USEPA and USGS conduct an assessment of the probable release history of groundwater contamination.[h]
April–May 2009	The USEPA and USGS conduct an assessment of the groundwater contamination.[h]
May 2010	The USEPA and USGS conduct an additional assessment of the CCP Site groundwater contamination.[h]

[a] Muskat and Neeley, 1985.

[b] Alabama Department of Public Health, 2004.

[c] Knowles and others, 1963.

[d] Black & Veatch, 2002.

[e] Scott and others, 1987.

[f] Malcolm Pirnie, Inc., 2003.

[g] Hall, 2007.

[h] This report.

Figure 4. Implied extent of perchloroethylene (PCE) in groundwater, Capital City Plume Site, Montgomery, Alabama, April 1991, May 1992, and October 1993.

EXPLANATION

Well and identifier—All wells are shown but not necessarily available for sampling between 1991 and 1993

9E ⦿   Public supply

MW-7I ●   Monitoring—S, shallow; I, intermediate

7.1 (April 1991)   PCE concentration in groundwater—In micrograms per liter, and date collected (modified from data in Black & Veatch, 2002)

⟶   Generalized groundwater-flow direction (modified from Hall, 2007)

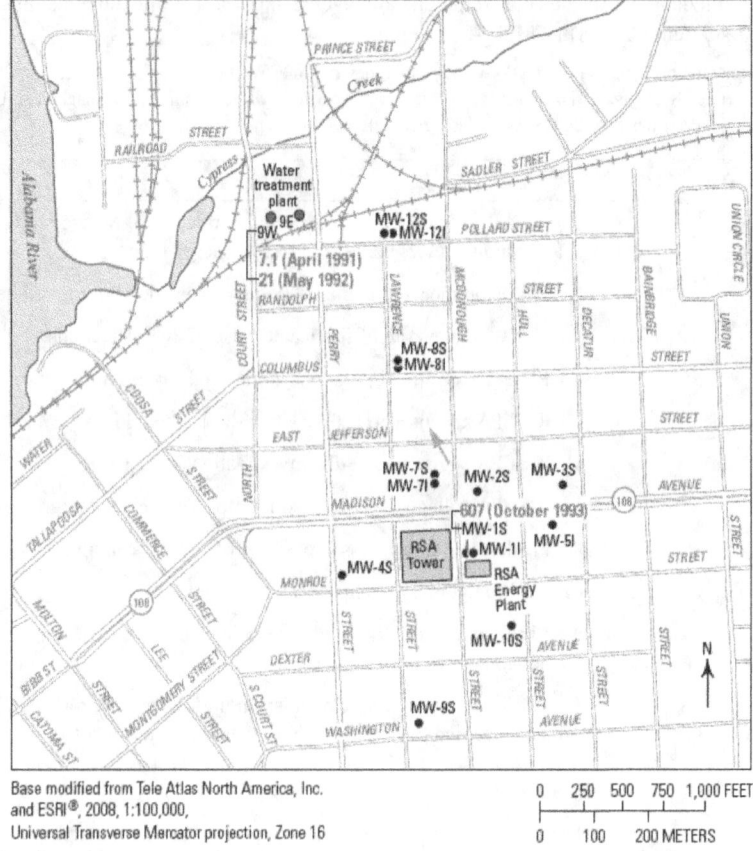

Base modified from Tele Atlas North America, Inc. and ESRI®, 2008, 1:100,000, Universal Transverse Mercator projection, Zone 16

and release history of the PCE were unknown. Pursuant to CERCLA regulations, in 2000 the USEPA initiated a Remedial Investigation (RI) to collect additional data to evaluate the extent of groundwater contamination at the CCP Site (Black & Veatch, 2002). A total of 16 permanent and 16 temporary monitoring wells were installed in the City of Montgomery using vibracore drilling technology. Most of the wells were installed adjacent to the RSA Energy Plant, near the contaminated public-supply wells, and between these locations of known contamination; at least two wells (MW-9S and MW-10S, fig. 3) were located upgradient of the RSA Energy Plant presumably to represent background conditions. Of the 16 permanent wells, 13 consisted of a pair of wells screened to the shallow and intermediate parts of the shallow aquifer (fig. 3; note that not all well pairs are shown because not all were sampled as part of the 2008–2010 study or the wells had been destroyed or were no longer accessible). Samples of soil and aquifer sediment were collected during well-drilling activities (Black & Veatch, 2002). During well drilling, visible contamination was not evident in the soil samples retrieved, and investigators concluded that a PCE source in the soil zone did not exist at the well locations (Black & Veatch, 2002). Slug tests were performed in the permanent monitoring wells, and the data were used to determine hydraulic conductivity of the shallow part of the

shallow aquifer. The calculated hydraulic conductivity and site hydraulic gradient were used to determine a groundwater-flow rate in the shallow part of the shallow aquifer of about 100 feet per year (ft/yr; Black & Veatch, 2002). The wells were sampled during May 2000, and the analytical results indicated PCE and TCE contamination (fig. 5); well 9W had detections of PCE and TCE at concentrations less than the method detection level (MDL) of 10 µg/L and, therefore, well 9W is not contoured as part of the PCE plume.

In January 2001, the USEPA collected additional soil and groundwater samples near the RSA Tower and Energy Plant areas (fig. 6); well 9W had detections of PCE and TCE at concentrations less than the MDL of 10 µg/L and, therefore, well 9W is not contoured as part of the PCE plume. Results of the soil samples supported previous observations of a lack of an obvious source of the PCE groundwater contamination (Black & Veatch, 2002).

In 2002, ADEM collected six surface-water samples from Cypress Creek—one sample collected near the mouth of Cypress Creek contained a PCE concentration of 7.2 µg/L (Black & Veatch, 2002). Of the 66 groundwater samples collected at the site that year, 55 samples had detections of chromium above the method reporting level (MRL), although little to no chromium was detected in the soil samples (Black & Veatch, 2002).

Figure 5. Implied extent of perchloro-ethylene (PCE) and trichloroethylene (TCE) in groundwater, Capital City Plume Site, Montgomery, Alabama, May 2000.

EXPLANATION

Well and identifier

9E ● Public supply

MW-7I ● Monitoring—S, shallow; I, intermediate. Wells shown in gray not installed until 2002

PCE concentration in groundwater, May 2000—In micrograms per liter (µg/L; modified from data in Black & Veatch, 2002). 10 µg/L was method detection level reported

85 Measured value, ≥10 µg/L; all other wells sampled but <10 ug/L

Estimated, ≥10 µg/L

TCE concentration in groundwater, May 2000—In µg/L (modified from data in Black & Veatch, 2002)

1 Measured value

⟹ **Generalized groundwater-flow direction** (modified from Hall, 2007)

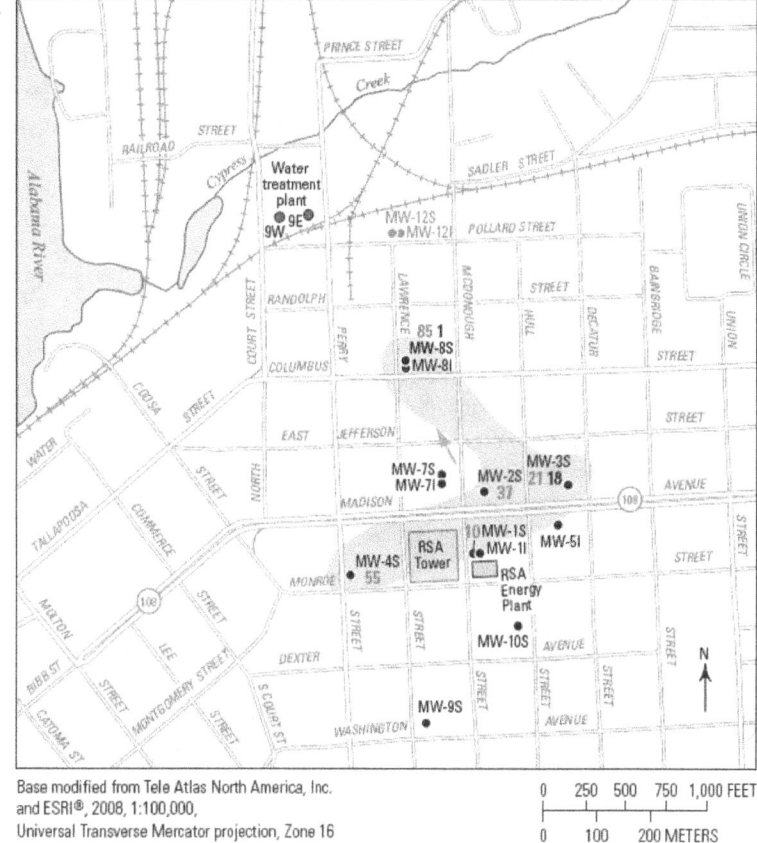

Base modified from Tele Atlas North America, Inc. and ESRI®, 2008, 1:100,000, Universal Transverse Mercator projection, Zone 16

0   250   500   750   1,000 FEET

0   100   200 METERS

Figure 6. Implied extent of perchloro-ethylene (PCE) and trichloroethylene (TCE) in groundwater, Capital City Plume Site, Montgomery, Alabama, January 2001.

EXPLANATION

Well and identifier

9E ● Public supply

MW-7I ● Monitoring—S, shallow; I, intermediate. Wells shown in gray not installed until 2002

PCE concentration in groundwater, January 2001—In micrograms per liter (µg/L; modified from data in Black & Veatch, 2002). 10 µg/L was method detection level reported

85 Measured value, ≥5 µg/L; all other wells sampled but <5 ug/L

Estimated, ≥10 µg/L

TCE concentration in groundwater, January 2001—In µg/L (modified from data in Black & Veatch, 2002)

2 Measured value

⟹ **Generalized groundwater-flow direction** (modified from Hall, 2007)

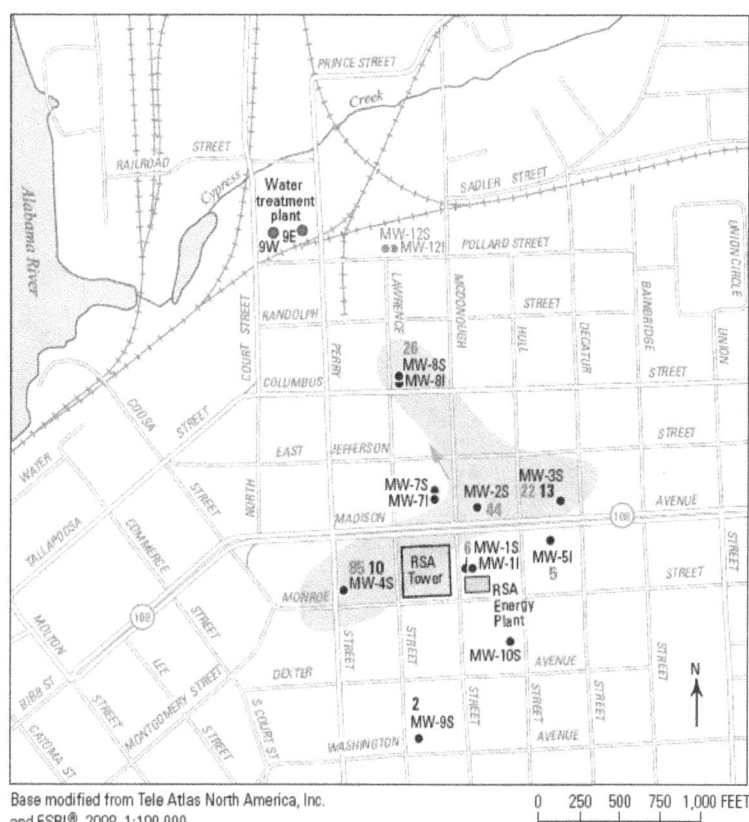

Base modified from Tele Atlas North America, Inc. and ESRI®, 2008, 1:100,000, Universal Transverse Mercator projection, Zone 16

0   250   500   750   1,000 FEET

0   100   200 METERS

In 2003, the City of Montgomery initiated a Feasibility Study at the CCP Site (Malcolm Pirnie, Inc., 2003). Additionally in 2003, an Environmental Site Assessment (ESA) was made on behalf of the Montgomery County Commission prior to the purchase of property located at the southeastern intersection of Washington Avenue and Lawrence Street because the property was located within the generalized boundary of the CCP Site (fig. 3), and was the former location of a commercial printing industry from 1940 to 1997. (In this report, a commercial printing industry is defined as those firms engaged in printing by one or more common processes, including those firms that publish newspapers, books, and periodicals, according to the Standard Industrial Classification Code Major Group 27— Printing, Publishing, and Allied Industry [U.S. Environmental Protection Agency, 1994, accessed on August 22, 2011, at *http://www.epa.gov/dfe/pubs/printing/cluster/*]). As part of the ESA, soil samples were collected from temporary borings,

and a hand-held total-gas detector with a photo-ionization detector (PID) was used to screen the samples in the field for VOC concentrations. Temporary wells also were installed and sampled (Environmental Materials Consultants, Inc., 2003). Soil and groundwater samples characterized by high VOC concentrations were sent for laboratory analysis, but the results indicated that no samples exceeded the MDL for PCE; benzene, toluene, ethylbenzene, and xylenes (BTEX); or methyl *tert*-butyl ether (MTBE). The samples were not analyzed for TCE. The source of the high VOC concentrations was not investigated further.

In July 2007, the City of Montgomery collected samples from the monitoring wells, and PCE and TCE concentrations continued to be detected in wells that previously had detections of PCE and TCE (fig. 7; Hall, 2007). Chromium also was detected in some wells (Hall, 2007). Well 9W was not sampled in July 2007.

Figure 7. Implied extent of perchloro-ethylene (PCE) and trichloroethylene (TCE) in groundwater, Capital City Plume Site, Montgomery, Alabama, July 2007.

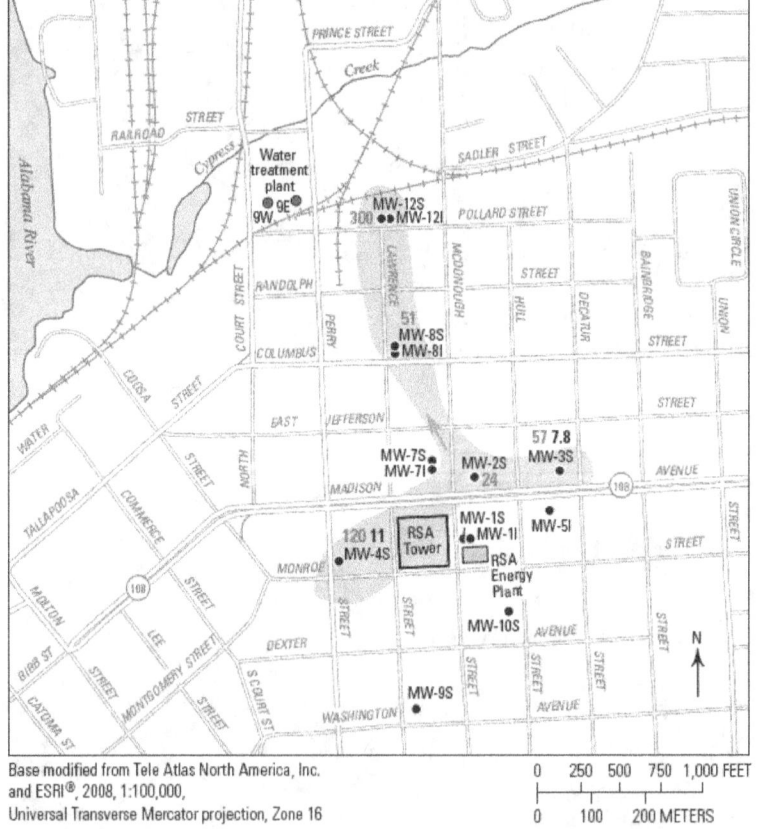

EXPLANATION

Well and identifier

9E ● Public supply

MW-7I ● Monitoring—S, shallow; I, intermediate

PCE concentration in groundwater, July 2007—In micrograms per liter (µg/L; modified from data in Hall, 2007)

51 Measured value, ≥5 µg/L; all other wells except well 9W sampled but <5 ug/L

Estimated, ≥5 µg/L

TCE concentration in groundwater, July 2007—In µg/L (modified from data in Hall, 2007)

11 Measured value

→ **Generalized groundwater-flow direction** (modified from Hall, 2007)

Base modified from Tele Atlas North America, Inc. and ESRI®, 2008, 1:100,000, Universal Transverse Mercator projection, Zone 16

0   250   500   750 1,000 FEET

0   100   200 METERS

Methods of Investigation

Multiple methods were used by the USEPA and USGS during 2008–2010 to investigate the potential source area, contamination pathway, and probable release history of PCE and TCE at the CCP Site. Most of these methods had not been used previously at the CCP Site and were selected to provide data to help the USEPA address the following questions that had remained unresolved since 1991:

1. What are the potential source areas of the PCE and TCE contamination in groundwater?

2. What are the predominant pathways that resulted in groundwater contamination?

3. What is the probable timeframe for groundwater contamination?

Because the City of Montgomery is an active metropolitan area, the site-assessment methods were selected to be as minimally invasive or disruptive as practicable. The methods used, therefore, are transferrable to other NPL or Superfund sites in urban areas characterized by groundwater contamination with unknown source areas or release histories.

Investigation of the Potential Source Area and Contamination Pathway

One obstacle that inhibited the ability of previous investigators to determine a potential source area of PCE-contaminated groundwater was the absence of PCE-contaminated soils near land surface in the areas investigated. Source-area determination was further complicated by the presence of (1) multiple past and current potential industrial or commercial sources of PCE within the City of Montgomery, (2) multiple land uses within the City of Montgomery since 1819, and (3) a lack of records documenting the use and disposal of hazardous materials prior to the 1980s.

Tree-Core Survey

In general, trees can be used to assess the distribution of subsurface contamination because tree roots interact with soil gas, soil moisture, and groundwater (Landmeyer, 2001; Vroblesky, 2008). Trees have been used by others to investigate chlorinated-solvent contamination of groundwater (Vroblesky and others, 1999; Landmeyer and others, 2000; Schumacher and others, 2004; Vroblesky and others, 2004; Vroblesky, 2008). Downtown Montgomery is characterized by landscape trees on city rights-of-way and are managed by the Urban Forester of Montgomery. The trees include laurel oak (*Quercus laurifolia*), live oak (*Quercus virginiana*), red oak (*Quercus ruba*), water oak (*Quercus nigra*), maple (*Acer rubrum*), ginkgo (*Ginkgo biloba*), and magnolia (*Magnolia grandiflora*) and range in age from about 10 to more than 100 yrs. The

grid-like distribution of city blocks and trees that overlie the approximate area of groundwater contamination provided an objective approach to guide the collection of tree cores for contaminant assessment (fig. 8). The city blocks selected for tree-core sampling are within the city's local groundwater drainage basin, as inferred from topographic highs, and are within or adjacent to the generalized boundary of the CCP Site.

Within the CCP Site, 69 trees were cored in and around downtown Montgomery (fig. 9) during August 2008, when transpiration rates are highest. Most of the trees cored were relatively young (less than [<] 50 yrs) but a few were greater than (>) 100 yrs. Not all blocks were included in the survey; some city blocks had no trees, or had trees that could not be cored because they were located on private or State property. Some trees were not cored at the request of the Urban Forester. Native trees, such as sycamore (*Platanus occidentalis*) and swamp cottonwood (*Populus heterophylla*) that grow in the riparian zones of the Alabama River and Cypress Creek, also were sampled. These trees were some of the largest and oldest trees sampled during the tree-core survey. Before tree-core sampling began, general information about each tree, such as genus, species, and diameter at breast height, was documented, and the location of each tree was mapped with a handheld global positioning system (Trimble® Nomad® 900 series) to an accuracy of within 6 ft.

All tree cores were collected with an increment auger using standard forestry practices (Phipps, 1985) and following methods of tree-core sampling for groundwater investigations presented in Vroblesky (2008). In brief, tree-core samples were collected at breast height from the southern side of each tree. Each core consisted of at least a 2-inch long cylinder-shaped sample of tissue that included the xylem (the water-transmitting part of the tree) and bark and represented a composite of the most recent annual growth rings. The core barrel was flame sterilized between sample collection. Cores were transferred as quickly as possible to 40-milliliter (mL) volatile organic analysis (VOA) glass vials, capped with a screw-on septated cap with a Teflon® liner to minimize contaminant loss by volatilization, and then stored on ice. Tree cores were analyzed for VOCs, such as PCE, TCE, and *cis*-1,2-dichloroethylene (*cis*-1,2-DCE), which had been previously detected in the groundwater (Black & Veatch, 2002), as well as the petroleum hydrocarbons benzene and toluene. The headspace of cores was analyzed by gas chromatography equipped with a photo-ionization detector (GC/PID; Photovac® 10S Plus®) in a climate-controlled room near the sampling area within a time span of minutes to 2 days after core sampling. The MRLs for PCE, TCE, *cis*-1,2-DCE, benzene, and toluene were 2, 20, 15, 10, and 10 parts per billion by volume (ppbv), respectively. For core samples analyzed on August 20, 2008, however, the MRL for TCE was 100 ppbv because of higher GC/PID baseline conditions that day. To increase contaminant volatilization into the vial headspace prior to GC/PID analysis, the vials were preheated in a microwave for between 8 and 30 seconds, as described in Vroblesky, Canova, and others (2009).

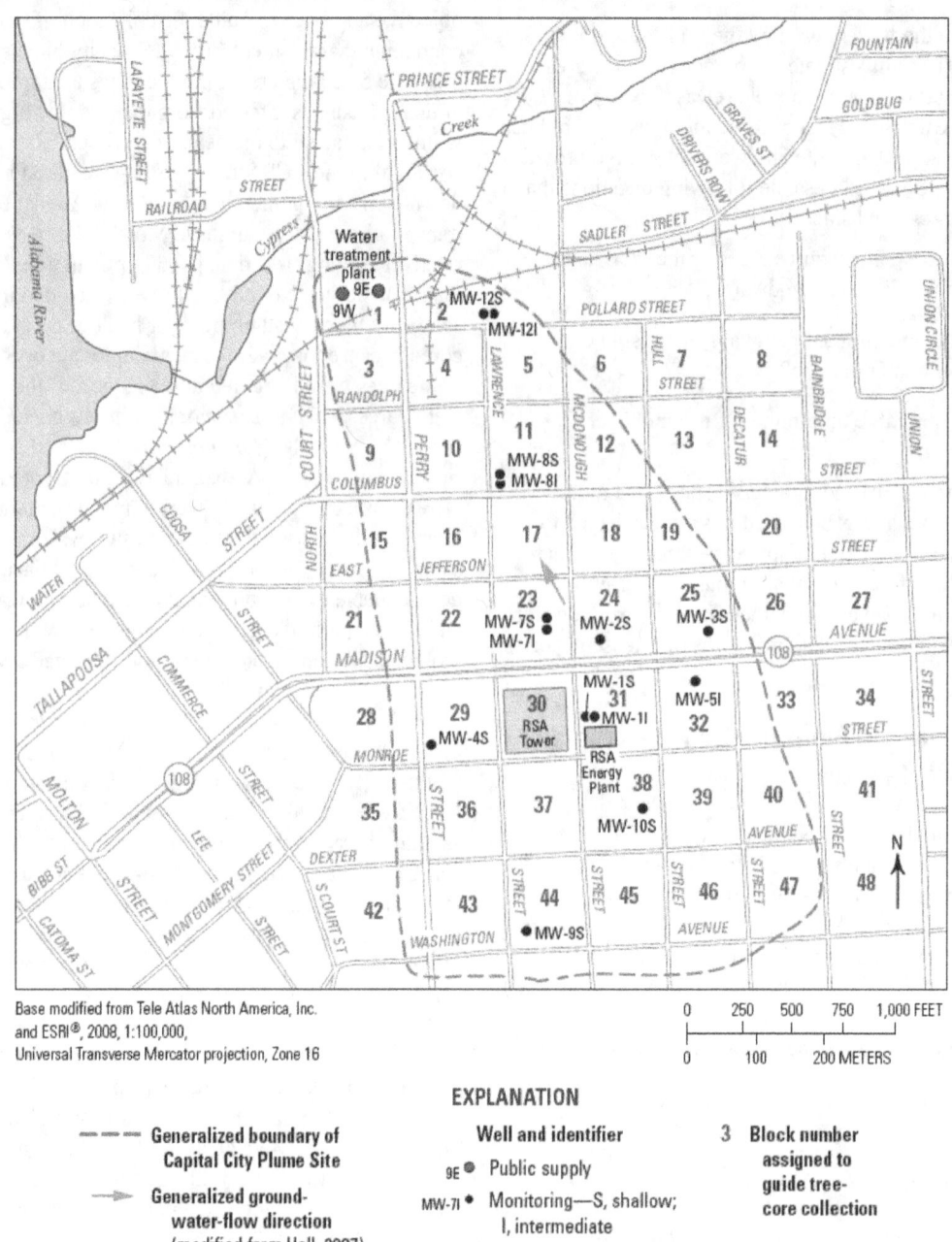

Base modified from Tele Atlas North America, Inc.
and ESRI®, 2008, 1:100,000,
Universal Transverse Mercator projection, Zone 16

0   250   500   750   1,000 FEET

0   100   200 METERS

EXPLANATION

– – – Generalized boundary of
          Capital City Plume Site

→   Generalized ground-
          water-flow direction
          (modified from Hall, 2007)

Well and identifier

9E ● Public supply

MW-7I ● Monitoring—S, shallow;
               I, intermediate

3   Block number
      assigned to
      guide tree-
      core collection

Figure 8.   Grid system to guide tree-core sampling in the vicinity of the Capital City Plume Site, Montgomery, Alabama, August 2008.

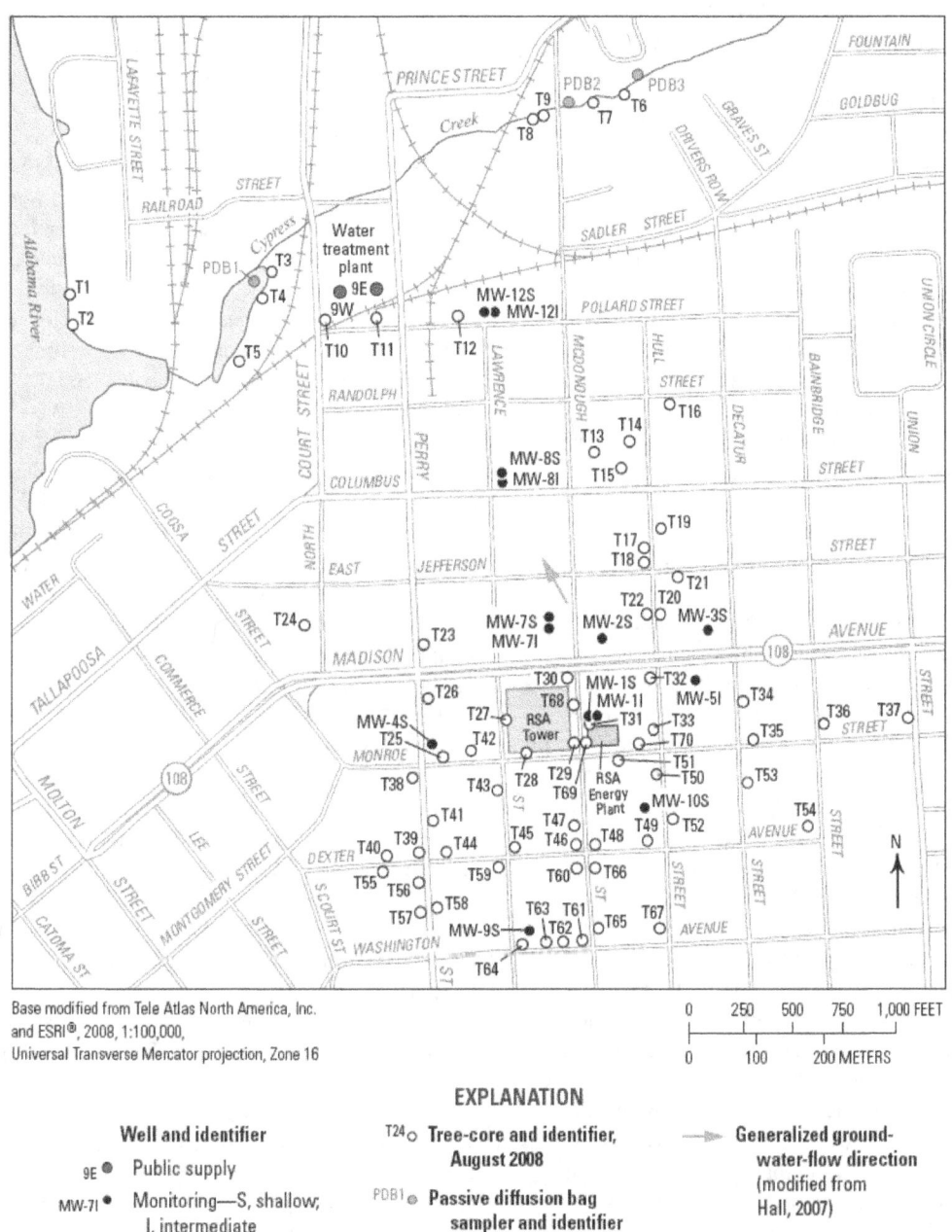

0   250   500   750   1,000 FEET

0   100   200 METERS

EXPLANATION

Well and identifier

9E ● Public supply

MW-7I ● Monitoring—S, shallow;
I, intermediate

T24 ○ **Tree-core and identifier,
August 2008**

PDB1 ◉ **Passive diffusion bag
sampler and identifier**

⟶ **Generalized ground-
water-flow direction
(modified from
Hall, 2007)**

Figure 9.   Locations of trees cored for analysis of volatile organic compounds (VOCs) and inorganic compounds, Capital City Plume Site, Montgomery, Alabama, and three passive diffusion bag (PDB) samplers in Cypress Creek, August 2008.

A subset of tree cores was shipped overnight to a contract laboratory (Elemental Analysis Incorporated) for analysis of inorganic compounds, such as chloride (used as a surrogate for past interaction of trees with sources of chloride, including chlorinated solvents), and sodium, by proton-induced x-ray emission (PIXE). Each core was cut down into a subsample of thickness greater than 80 microns for PIXE thick-target analysis. Tree cores have been analyzed for inorganic compounds for many years using this method, and the analysis is applicable for most major trace elements (Lewis, 1995). Tree cores that are representative of urban conditions in the southern United States not affected by chlorinated-solvent-contaminated groundwater were collected near the USGS South Carolina Water Science Center in Columbia. The PIXE calibration, accuracy, precision, and detection limits for individual trace elements, such as chloride and sodium, are contained in the laboratory's quality assurance document (Elemental Analysis Incorporated, 2008).

Groundwater Sampling and Analysis

During April–May 2009, groundwater samples were collected by the USGS from 13 CCP Site monitoring wells believed to be representative of site conditions by the USEPA. Data collected at each well included measurement of the static groundwater levels with an electric tape prior to sample collection. Groundwater samples were collected from the mid-point of the screened interval by using Teflon® tubing and a Fultz dedicated submersible pump with low-flow techniques following USGS sampling protocols reported in the USGS National Field Manual (U.S. Geological Survey, variously dated). Physical properties and chemical constituents of groundwater, such as temperature, dissolved oxygen (DO), specific conductance (SC), and pH, were measured using a YSI 6920® sonde (YSI, Inc.) in a flow-through cell during groundwater sample collection. The sonde was calibrated each day of sampling by using appropriate standard methods for DO, SC and pH as reported in the USGS National Field Manual (U.S. Geological Survey, variously dated). Wet-chemistry Hach® kits (Hach Company) also were used in the field during sampling to measure DO, ferrous iron, nitrate, sulfate, sulfide, and turbidity.

Groundwater samples were collected only after the variability for a specific physical property did not exceed an established criterion that was operationally defined for a set of about five sequential measurements, as reported in the USGS National Field Manual (U.S. Geological Survey, variously dated). Groundwater samples for inorganic compound analysis were collected first. These samples were not filtered because of the low turbidity (<5 nephelometric turbidity units, NTU) of the groundwater being pumped. Groundwater samples collected for inorganic analysis were preserved with nitric acid (Ultrex grade 7.7 Normal) to a pH of 2, stored on ice, and shipped to the USGS National Water Quality Laboratory (NWQL) in

Denver, Colorado, for analysis. Then groundwater samples for VOC analysis were collected, preserved with a 1:1 solution of hydrochloric acid to a pH of 2, stored on ice, and shipped to the USGS NWQL for analysis. During sampling, two field-blank samples (one for inorganic compounds, and one for VOCs) and one replicate sample were collected at well MW-1I. To reduce the possibility of cross contamination, the pump was decontaminated between wells by scrubbing with soapy water (Liqui-Nox® and distilled water) and rinsing with tap water, deionized water, and methanol, after which the equipment was allowed to air dry. The pump wiring was decontaminated in the same manner, but without the methanol rinse except for wiring nearest the pump. The Teflon® tubing was replaced with new tubing between wells.

Groundwater samples were collected by the USEPA from the same 13 monitoring wells during May 2010 as part of a USEPA-conducted sampling event (Scott Miller, U.S. Environmental Protection Agency, oral commun., June 2010). As part of this sampling event, the USGS collected separate groundwater samples for sulfur hexafluoride (SF_6) and chlorofluorocarbon (CFC) analyses using the methods described above with the following modifications. To ensure that the groundwater samples did not come into contact with air during sampling, the sample vials (250-mL glass vials) were filled beneath a volume of groundwater pumped from the well into a bucket. The sample tubing, made of nylon to eliminate contact of the sample with air during pumping, was placed in each vial under water; the vial was allowed to overflow, and then each vial was capped under water using a metal screw cap with an aluminum foil liner. The samples then were removed from the bucket, checked for the presence of air bubbles, and sealed with electrical tape around the bottle caps. The sample bottles were not stored on ice but were shipped directly to the USGS Chlorofluorocarbon Laboratory in Reston, Virginia. The concentrations of SF_6 and CFCs detected in the groundwater samples were used to interpret the recharge age of the groundwater prior to the sampling date, based on a piston-type flow model according to Plummer and Friedman (1999).

During August 2008, three PDB samplers were installed less than 1 ft into the hyporheic zone of Cypress Creek (fig. 9). The PDB sampler consisted of a 40 mL VOA vial wrapped in plastic and was prepared and installed according to the method described in Church and others (2002). After exposure of the PDB samplers to the groundwater in the hyporheic zone for no more than 6 hours, the PDB samplers were retrieved, capped with a screw-on septated cap with a Teflon® liner, and analyzed by using GC/PID as described above for the tree-core samples.

The City of Montgomery has a long history of multiple land uses since its incorporation on December 3, 1819. The USEPA used historic Sanborn insurance maps, USGS topographic maps, historical maps from the University of Alabama Department of Geography, and maps in books featuring the City of Montgomery to delineate former land uses within the CCP Site.

Investigation of the Probable Release History

Various methods were used during 2008–2010 to investigate the probable release history of the PCE and TCE detected in groundwater at the CCP Site. The methods used included measurement of the concentrations of naturally emplaced hydrologic tracers, such as CFCs and SF_6, which had not been measured previously.

Sulfur Hexafluoride and Chlorofluorocarbon Concentrations and Estimated Recharge Dates

Sulfur hexafluoride is a gas present at trace levels in the atmosphere from natural and anthropogenic sources. In general, detections of SF_6 in groundwater indicate the presence of water recharged since the 1970s, because substantial production of SF_6, and release to the atmosphere and introduction into the hydrosphere did not begin until the late 1960s (Busenberg and Plummer, 1997; Busenberg and Plummer, 2000). The USGS collected groundwater samples for analysis of SF_6 concentrations during the USEPA's May 2010 sampling event. These groundwater samples were analyzed by the USGS Chlorofluorocarbon Laboratory in Reston, Virginia.

Detections of 1,1,2-trichloro-1,2,2-trifluoroethane (CFC-113) and trichlorofluoromethane (CFC-11) in groundwater indicate either (1) ambient concentrations representative of recently recharged shallow groundwater or (2) a localized source of CFC contamination (Plummer and Friedman, 1999). The groundwater samples collected by the USGS during the USEPA's May 2010 sampling event were obtained by using CFC-specific sampling techniques that include isolation of the sample bottle from the atmosphere during sample collection, as previously described.

Dendrochemistry

The study of annual growth rings of trees, or dendrochronology, has been used for almost 100 yrs to reconstruct and describe the past climate and history of hydrologic conditions at sites where trees grow (Ferguson and Graybill, 1983; Lewis, 1995). Dendrochronology is based on the fact that, for most trees, each year of growth is preserved as an annual concentric ring of tissue that reflects the environmental factors surrounding a tree as it grew. The preservation of environmental factors in growth rings of trees at contaminated sites also have been used to investigate the interaction of plants with trace metals (Nabais and others, 1999; Balouet and Oudijk, 2006; Balouet and others, 2007; Balouet and others, 2009), which is referred to as dendrochemistry. Contaminant exposure preserved in annual growth rings can be analyzed to determine the timing of exposure. This approach was used by Vroblesky and Yanosky (1990) to determine when heavy metals had been released to groundwater at a landfill site in Maryland. Such retrospective analysis was used to understand the interactions of plants with heavy metals, such as zinc and lead, that have been released to the subsurface (Lewis, 1995) and, in the case of iron, released to the air (Baes and McLaughlin, 1984). Typically, dendrochemical approaches are not supported for use with organic compounds, because the organic molecules are not preserved in the plant tissue after uptake. However, organic compounds that are halogenated, such as PCE and TCE, can be identified in dendrochemistry because the chlorine substitution is preserved in the tree as a spike in chloride concentration in the growth ring(s) formed during interaction with the contamination (Yanosky and others, 2001). Moreover, the detection of chloride in trees was used to attribute release events from source areas at multiple sites (Burken and others, 2011).

For all dendrochemical approaches, older annual tree rings are assumed to have lost biological function and, therefore, preserve trace elements within the ring at concentrations equal to when the element was originally incorporated. Dendrochemistry was used at the CCP Site to investigate when particular trees near suspected source areas were exposed to subsurface chlorinated solvents. Trees sampled during August 2008 and determined to contain detections of chlorinated solvents were re-sampled during January 2009 for chloride and sodium concentrations by using the same field techniques and PIXE analysis, as previously described. For trees known to be growing in or near suspected source areas, the detection of chloride in specific and datable annual growth rings counting in from the bark was used to constrain probable times of contaminant uptake and, as a result, the probable contaminant-release history. For trees growing some distance from suspected source areas, the detection of chloride in annual growth rings indicates the earliest date when groundwater or unsaturated-zone contamination interacted with the trees at a particular location. The tree-core concentration of sodium enabled an examination of chloride-to-sodium ratios as an estimate of trends in sources or sinks of chloride.

The assumption that tree rings preserve an accurate record of the past uptake of trace elements is not necessarily valid in all cases. Some elements after uptake can be translocated to previously formed rings (Nabais and others, 1999). If trace element concentrations within each ring change over time after uptake, it complicates the use of these elements to date contaminant releases (Hagemeyer and Schäfer, 1995). Hagemeyer and Schäfer (1995) identified considerable seasonal variability in concentrations of the metals cadmium, lead, and zinc in beech trees, with the highest concentrations occurring in tree rings during dormancy when the water content in trees is higher than during periods of active growth. Hagemeyer and others (1994) also detected seasonal variations in nickel concentrations in the stem wood of beech trees. Baes and McLaughlin (1984) reported that aluminum, calcium, copper, manganese, and zinc are not translocated after uptake, whereas lead may be translocated (Baes and Ragsdale, 1981).

Investigation of the Potential Source Area and Contamination Pathway

The results of VOC detections in cores collected from 69 landscape trees in and around downtown Montgomery and in native vegetation growing in the riparian zones of the Alabama River and Cypress Creek are presented in this section. Analytical results of inorganic compounds detected in 17 trees also are presented, as are the groundwater-sampling results for 13 monitoring wells during April–May 2009. Past land uses within the CCP Site also are discussed. These data were collected to help investigate the potential contamination source area and pathway at the CCP Site.

Tree-Core Survey

In August 2008, cores were collected from 69 landscape trees in and around Montgomery and in riparian zones (fig. 9; table 2, at the back of this report). The results of the detection of the chlorinated solvents PCE, TCE, and cis-1,2-DCE and the petroleum hydrocarbons benzene and toluene as measured in these cores are presented in this section of the report.

Volatile Organic Compounds

The chlorinated solvents PCE, TCE, and cis-1,2-DCE were detected in the vial headspace at concentrations greater than the MRL for each analyte (table 2). Of the 69 trees cored, TCE was the most frequently detected compound above the MRL and was detected in 24 trees (34 percent); PCE was the next most frequently detected compound above the MRL and was detected in 7 trees (10 percent); cis-1,2-DCE was detected above the MRL in 2 trees (3 percent). Both PCE and TCE were detected in 5 trees, and both TCE and cis-1,2-DCE were detected in 2 trees; cis-1,2-DCE was not detected in any tree that also contained PCE. The petroleum hydrocarbons benzene and toluene were detected above the MRL in only trees T53 and T54.

The highest concentration of PCE measured during August 2008 (8,782 ppbv) was for one of two tree-core samples collected from tree 32 (T32; fig. 10), which is located on the same block as the RSA Energy Plant where PCE was first detected in 1993 in soil-gas and groundwater samples. Nearby and adjacent to the RSA Energy Plant, PCE and TCE were detected in core samples from tree 31 (T31). Detection of PCE and TCE in tree cores from this area of well documented PCE- and TCE-contaminated groundwater validates the use of the tree-core survey approach in detecting contaminants in the subsurface at this site, as has been shown previously for other sites (Vroblesky and others, 1999; Landmeyer and others, 2000; Schumacher and others, 2004; Vroblesky and others, 2004; Vroblesky, 2008). The highest concentration of TCE (68,650 ppbv) was measured in a core sample from tree 64 (T64), which is at the northeastern intersection of

Washington Avenue and Lawrence Street in an area of the CCP Site that was not previously characterized by TCE contamination and adjacent to the former location of a commercial printing industry from 1940 to 1997 (fig. 10). The depth to groundwater measured in well MW-9S near T64 at the time of tree-core sampling was about 56 ft below land surface, much deeper than the depth penetration by roots of oak trees; therefore, the detection of TCE in the T64 core sample indicates a source of TCE in the unsaturated zone at this location.

The detection of PCE and TCE in the headspace of vials that contained tree-core samples from these locations (T31, T32, and T64) indicates the presence of

1. A near-surface residual source of PCE and TCE,

2. A source of PCE and TCE in groundwater from the shallow aquifer, or

3. A mixture of both sources.

The spatial distribution of the trees that had detections of PCE and TCE during August 2008 (fig. 10) includes trees (T12, T22, and T38) that are growing in the area of PCE- and TCE-contaminated groundwater as delineated in July 2007 (Hall, 2007). PCE also was detected in trees growing in areas downgradient of this area in the riparian zones of Cypress Creek and the Alabama River (T2, T3, T5, T6, T7, and T8, fig. 10). PCE and TCE also were detected in tree cores from areas where no monitoring wells were located, such as T14, T17, T18, and T19. The petroleum hydrocarbons benzene and toluene were detected above the MRL only in trees T53 and T54 located east of Decatur Street, and these trees did not contain PCE or TCE. More importantly, however, multiple trees that had detections of either PCE, TCE, or both (T28, T29, T31, T33, T35, T39, T41, T43, T47, T61, and T64) are located upgradient from the area of previously identified PCE- and TCE-contaminated groundwater near the RSA Energy Plant (figs. 7, 10, the delineated distribution of PCE concentrations in groundwater identified by Hall [2007]). This detection of PCE and TCE in tree cores provides the first evidence that a potential source of the groundwater contamination could be upgradient along Dexter and Washington Avenues. In general, cis-1,2-DCE was detected only in samples from T64 and T6 (fig. 10) and was not detected in samples from trees growing near well MW-4S, in which cis-1,2-DCE was detected during July 2007 (Hall, 2007) (fig. 7).

The high detections of TCE in the T64 cores during August 2008 also shed light on results from two investigations, described previously, and conducted within the extent of the CCP Site near T64. During the RI conducted during 2000, field personnel used a field-portable flame-ionization detector (FID) to survey sediment collected during vibracore installation of monitoring wells. The FID results indicated the presence of total hydrocarbon in concentrations of 10 to 300 parts per million (ppm) and 10 to 80 ppm in cores of sediment removed between land surface and 40 ft below land surface but above the water table for wells MW-9S and MW-10S, respectively, both upgradient of the PCE- and

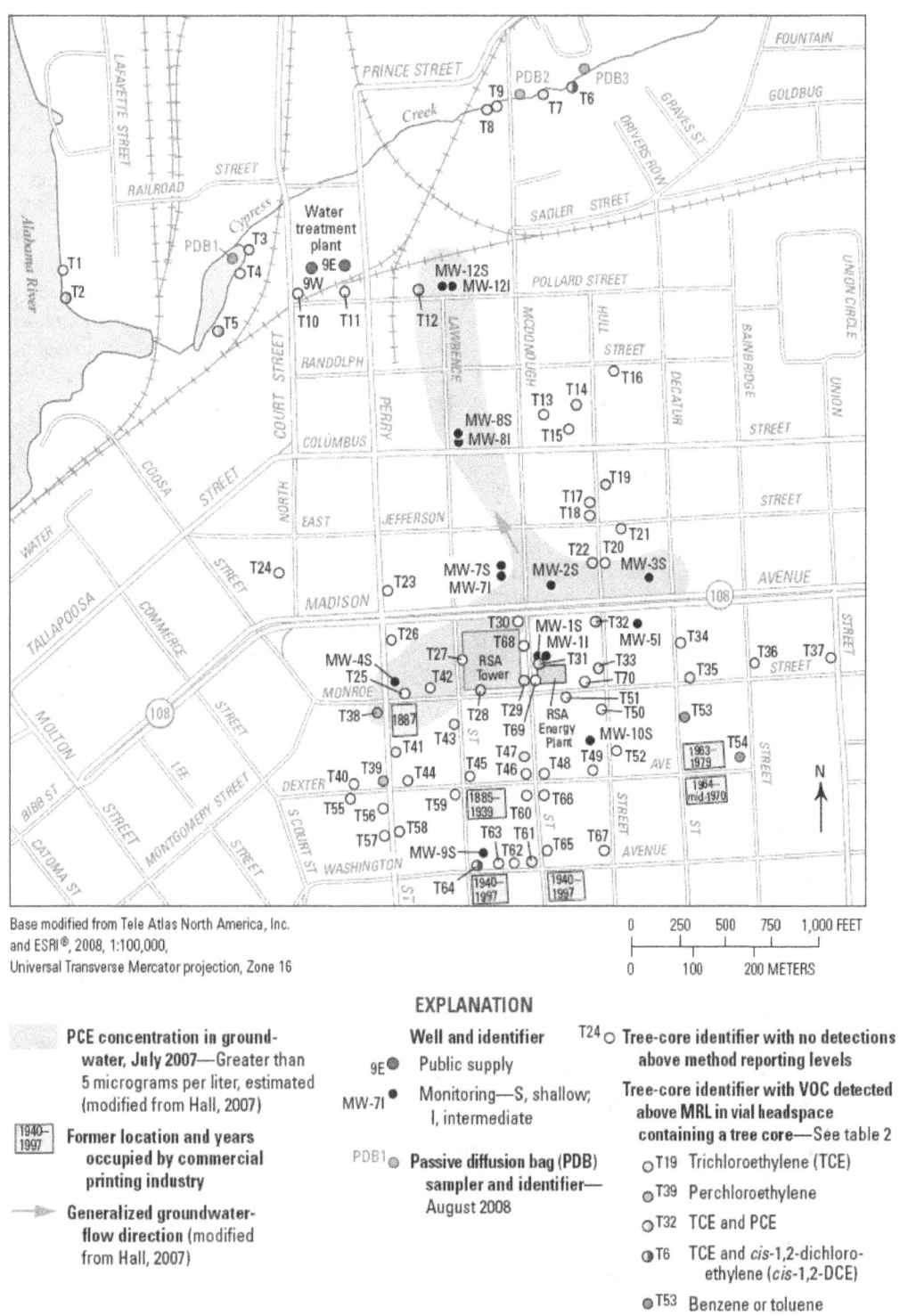

Base modified from Tele Atlas North America, Inc.
and ESRI®, 2008, 1:100,000,
Universal Transverse Mercator projection, Zone 16

0   250   500   750   1,000 FEET

0   100   200 METERS

EXPLANATION

PCE concentration in groundwater, July 2007—Greater than
5 micrograms per liter, estimated
(modified from Hall, 2007)

1940–
1997   Former location and years
occupied by commercial
printing industry

Generalized groundwater-
flow direction (modified
from Hall, 2007)

Well and identifier

9E●   Public supply

MW-7I●   Monitoring—S, shallow;
I, intermediate

PDB1●   Passive diffusion bag (PDB)
sampler and identifier—
August 2008

T24○   Tree-core identifier with no detections
above method reporting levels

Tree-core identifier with VOC detected
above MRL in vial headspace
containing a tree core—See table 2

○T19   Trichloroethylene (TCE)

○T39   Perchloroethylene

○T32   TCE and PCE

◐T6   TCE and cis-1,2-dichloro-
ethylene (cis-1,2-DCE)

●T53   Benzene or toluene

Figure 10.   Locations of trees cored during August 2008, trees with volatile organic compound (VOC)
detections above the method reporting level (MRL) in the tree-core headspace, former commercial printing
industry sites, generalized direction of groundwater flow in the shallow aquifer, and delineated area of
perchloroethylene (PCE) concentrations measured in groundwater during July 2007, Capital City Plume
Site, Montgomery, Alabama.

TCE-contaminated groundwater (figs. 10,11; data from Black & Veatch, 2002; data interpretation by U.S. Geological Survey). These ranges of total hydrocarbon concentrations in sediment above the water table, when combined with the measured high concentration of TCE in the headspace of a tree-core sample from nearby tree T64, indicate the presence of near-surface contamination. Conversely, FID measurements in sediment above the water table for downgradient wells MW-1S (near the area of workers' acute exposure to vapors during September 1993) and MW-4S did not exceed 100 ppm, and did not exceed 300 ppm for well MW-8S (fig. 11; data from Black & Veatch, 2002; data interpretation by U.S. Geological Survey). In 2003, the previously described ESA indicated that although high readings were measured for some soil samples screened with a PID, none of the samples submitted to a laboratory exceeded the MDL of 5 parts per billion for PCE, BTEX, and MTBE, and the samples were not analyzed for TCE (Environmental Materials Consultants, Inc., 2003). Moreover, during the RI conducted in 2000, sediments cored from 120 ft below land surface in the intermediate part of the shallow aquifer at well MW-1I had FID results for total hydrocarbon concentrations that exceeded 1,000 ppm). Sediments cored from 65 ft below land surface at well MW-7I had detections near 150 ppm. Combined, these detections indicate the occurrence of contamination in the intermediate part of the shallow aquifer at these locations (fig. 10).

The distribution of trees with detections of chlorinated solvents during the August 2008 tree-core survey were compared to former locations of multiple, historical land-use activities within the CCP Site that may have used these chemicals since 1842. Multiple activities that may have included the use of PCE and TCE include dry cleaners, metal shops, gasoline stations, and printing operations of various sizes. Surveys conducted by the USEPA of past activities performed indicated that dry cleaning was not performed at the CCP Site and no releases from gasoline stations had been reported (Scott Miller, U.S. Environmental Protection Agency, oral commun., February 12, 2009). The commercial printing industry, however, has occupied multiple locations within the extent of the CCP Site in downtown Montgomery since at least 1828 (table 1). For example, a newspaper printing operation occupied multiple locations in downtown Montgomery and within the extent of the CCP Site from 1833 to 1997. This commercial printing industry has been located in areas where PCE and TCE contamination was detected in tree cores (fig. 10). Moreover, the location of this newspaper printing operation between 1940 and 1997 along Washington Avenue and the location of separate printing operations to the east along Dexter Avenue between 1963 and 1979 currently (2011) represent the only identified potential upgradient sources of the PCE and TCE detected in the adjacent trees and in groundwater from nearby or downgradient monitoring wells.

Chloride

Chloride was detected above the mean MDL of 5.95 milligrams per kilogram (mg/kg, equivalent to ppm) in 13 of 17 trees that represent subsurface conditions across the CCP Site (table 3). Chloride concentrations differed widely among trees cored and ranged from 4.0 to 135.4 mg/kg; the mean concentration was 31.84 mg/kg. Chloride concentrations above the mean were detected in 7 trees—T3, T23, T29, T31, T35, T47, and T59 (fig. 12). The trees with elevated chloride concentrations are downgradient from Washington Avenues and, except for T59, Dexter Avenue; these trees, except for T23 and T59, also had TCE detections. A similar relation between chloride in tree cores and TCE contamination was reported by Yanosky and others (2001) for another study area characterized by chlorinated-solvent contamination.

Table 3. Tree-core sampling results for chloride and sodium concentrations and the chloride-to-sodium ratios, Capital City Plume Site, Montgomery, Alabama, August 2008.

[ID, identification; mg/kg, milligram per kilogram (equivalent to ppm, parts per million); Cl:Na, chloride-to-sodium ratio; NA, not applicable; R, replicate]

Tree ID (fig. 12)	Tree diameter (inches)	Chloride (mg/kg)	Sodium (mg/kg)	Cl:Na
Mean method detection level	NA	5.95	67.10	NA
T59	22	49.43	63.80	0.77
T29	8	31.85	63.80	0.49
T15	44	29.83	60.20	0.49
T64	28	27.59	66.60	0.40
T23	7	135.40	68.00	1.90
T25	13	4.00	65.00	0.06
T47	20	31.80	70.00	0.44
T31	26	32.11	67.00	0.47
T44	19	4.20	66.00	0.06
T17	13	5.10	74.00	0.06
T3	23	44.00	65.00	0.67
T6	17	12.76	66.00	0.18
T21	17	26.96	68.00	0.38
T35	12	68.03	71.00	0.95
T40	22	4.20	68.00	0.06
T32	14	29.20	66.00	0.43
T32(R)	14	19.71	75.00	0.25
T62	23	16.90	59.00	0.27
Mean, all tree cores (mg/kg)	NA	31.84	66.80	NA

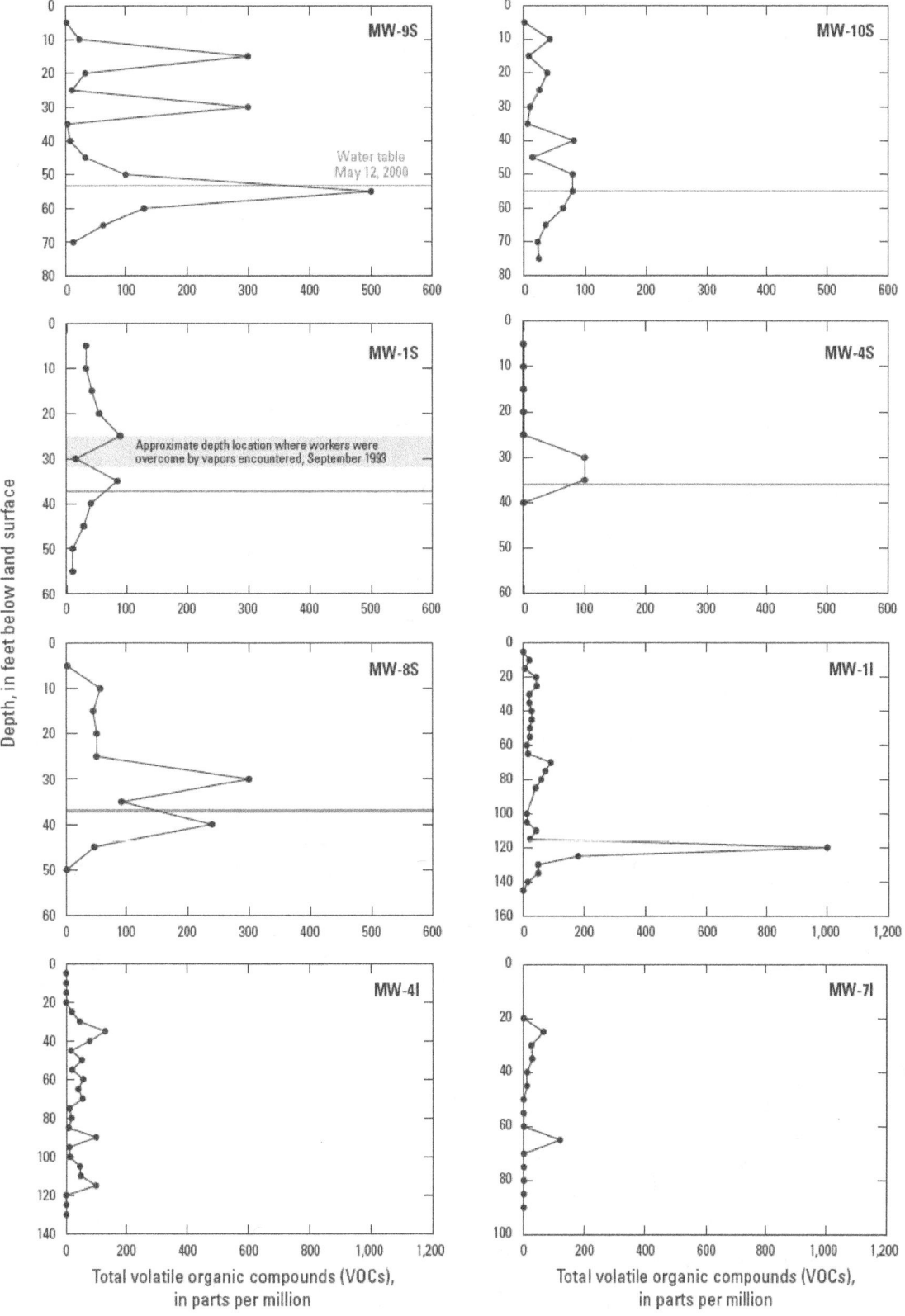

Figure 11. Results of flame ionization detector (FID) screening of sediment cored during installation of monitoring wells MW-9S, MW-10S, MW-1S, MW-4S, MW-8S, MW-1I, MW-4I, and MW-7I, Capital City Plume Site, Montgomery, Alabama, 2000 (data from Black & Veatch, 2002; data interpretation by U.S. Geological Survey; scales vary).

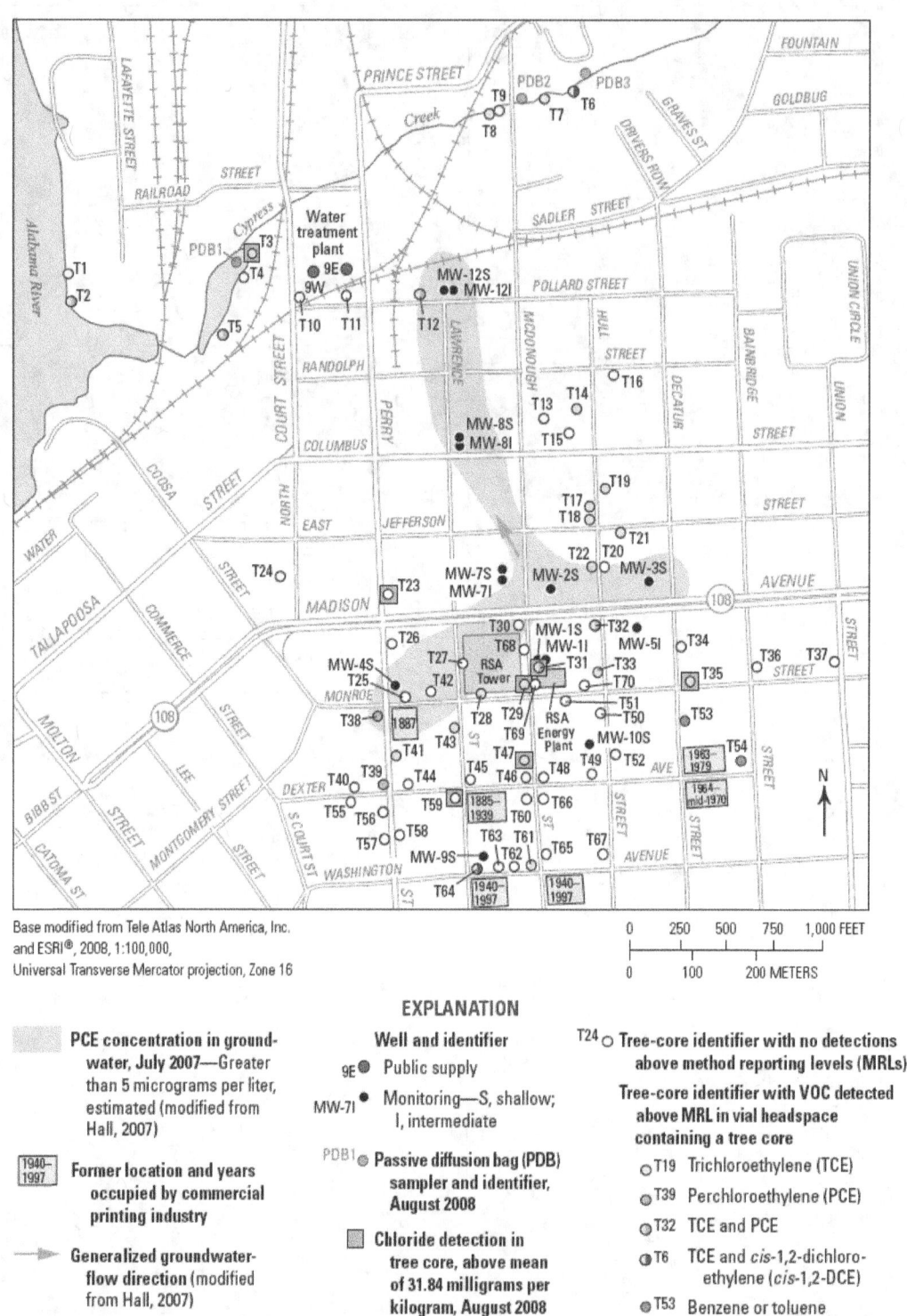

Base modified from Tele Atlas North America, Inc.
and ESRI®, 2008, 1:100,000,
Universal Transverse Mercator projection, Zone 16

0   250   500   750   1,000 FEET

0   100   200 METERS

EXPLANATION

PCE concentration in groundwater, July 2007—Greater
than 5 micrograms per liter,
estimated (modified from
Hall, 2007)

1940–
1997   Former location and years
occupied by commercial
printing industry

Generalized groundwater-
flow direction (modified
from Hall, 2007)

Well and identifier

9E ● Public supply

MW-7I ● Monitoring—S, shallow;
I, intermediate

PDB1 ◉ Passive diffusion bag (PDB)
sampler and identifier,
August 2008

Chloride detection in
tree core, above mean
of 31.84 milligrams per
kilogram, August 2008

T24 ○ Tree-core identifier with no detections
above method reporting levels (MRLs)

Tree-core identifier with VOC detected
above MRL in vial headspace
containing a tree core

○T19 Trichloroethylene (TCE)

◐T39 Perchloroethylene (PCE)

◑T32 TCE and PCE

◔T6 TCE and cis-1,2-dichloro-
ethylene (cis-1,2-DCE)

●T53 Benzene or toluene

Figure 12.   Locations of trees that had chloride detections exceeding the mean of 31.84 milligrams per
kilogram in co e samples, Capital City Plume Site, Montgomery, Alabama, August 2008.

The detection of elevated levels of chloride in tree cores is important because it could indicate past, recent, or cumulative interaction of trees with a source of elevated chloride, such as chlorinated solvents.

Sodium was detected above the mean MDL of 67.1 mg/kg in seven samples (table 3). The sodium concentrations were relatively similar among the trees cored and ranged from 59 to 75 mg/kg; the mean was 66.8 mg/kg. Comparison of the chloride (Cl) to sodium (Na) ratio (Cl:Na) of the tree cores indicates that the ratio was greater than 1 for only one sample, which was collected from T23. A ratio greater than 1 would indicate an imbalance in the sources and sinks of chloride and sodium, such as a source of chloride or a sink of sodium, or a differential uptake rate for each inorganic compound. Concentrations of chloride and sodium also were measured in trees sampled during 2009 in Columbia, South Carolina, which is a similar urban capital city in the southeastern United States (data not shown). All of the trees cored in the Columbia area contained chloride, but the highest concentration was 66 mg/kg, half the highest chloride concentration measured in tree cores sampled at the CCP Site.

Groundwater Sampling and Analysis

Groundwater samples were collected by the USGS during April–May 2009 to document any changes in flow direction and concentrations since the last round of groundwater sampling conducted in July 2007 (Hall, 2007) and to determine if the detection of PCE and TCE in tree cores during August 2008 could be explained further by the detection of PCE and TCE in groundwater. Results of groundwater levels, flow direction, analyses for redox-sensitive chemical properties (for example, DO, sulfide, sulfate, and nitrate) and measurements of physical properties (turbidity, SC, and pH) are presented. The groundwater samples collected as part of the May 2010 sampling event conducted by the USEPA are described later in this report.

During April–May 2009, the depth to groundwater and direction of flow generally were similar to what had been previously reported. In both the shallow and intermediate parts of the shallow aquifer, groundwater flows to the north-northwest toward Cypress Creek and the Alabama River (fig. 13). The altitude of groundwater in wells MW-1I and MW-8I were slightly lower than the altitude of groundwater measured in the shallower of the well pairs (MW-1S and MW-8S), which indicates a potential downward vertical head gradient at these locations. The converse scenario, one of potential upward vertical head gradient, is indicated at wells MW-7I and MW-12I (fig. 13B).

Groundwater sampled from the shallow part of the shallow aquifer was characterized by oxic reduction/oxidation (redox) conditions. DO concentrations ranged from 4 to 6.4 milligrams per liter (mg/L) when measured using the Hach® method, and from 2.6 to 6.6 mg/L when measured with the YSI® multiparameter sonde (table 4). Groundwater samples from the shallow part of the shallow aquifer contained between 4 and 19 mg/L sulfate, between 1.5 and 7.1 mg/L nitrate, and between 0.01 and 0.05 mg/L ferrous iron. Turbidity ranged from 0.1 to 1.3 NTUs. SC ranged from 70 to 322 microsiemens per centimeter (µS/cm), and pH ranged from 5 to 7.3. Groundwater sampled from the intermediate part of the shallow aquifer also was characterized by oxic redox conditions. DO concentrations ranged from 2.2 to 6.6 mg/L when measured using the Hach® method, and from 1.8 to 6.9 mg/L when measured with a DO-probe attached to the multiparameter sonde (table 4). Samples from the intermediate part of the shallow aquifer contained concentrations of sulfate between 1 and 6 mg/L, nitrate between 0.7 and 6.6 mg/L, and ferrous iron between 0.01 and 0.12 mg/L. Turbidity ranged from 0.6 to 3.61 NTUs, SC ranged from 60 to 212 µS/cm, and pH ranged from 5.2 to 7.7. The presence of oxic conditions throughout the shallow aquifer at the CCP Site inhibits the reductive dechlorination of chlorinated solvents and, therefore, partially explains the continued presence of PCE and TCE in groundwater since initial detection in 1991.

Results for VOCs detected in monitoring wells at the CCP Site during April–May 2009 are listed in table 5, and the distributions of selected VOCs related to the CCP Site are shown in figure 14. For wells screened to the shallow part of the shallow aquifer, PCE was detected above the NPDWR MCL of 5 µg/L in wells MW-1S (5.28 µg/L), MW-2S (25.0 µg/L), MW-4S (84.8 µg/L), MW-8S (18.8 µg/L), and MW-12S (63.8 µg/L; table 5; fig. 14A). PCE was estimated at concentrations above the MRL of 0.04 µg/L in wells MW-7S and MW-10S; the concentration was estimated because the value was extrapolated below the lowest calibration range. PCE was estimated to be 0.03 µg/L in well MW-9S; the concentration was estimated because the value was below the MRL. TCE was detected above the NPDWR MCL of 5 µg/L in MW-4S, which also had the highest PCE concentration. TCE was detected above the MRL of 0.02 µg/L in all wells except MW-7S and MW-10S. The transformation byproducts of PCE and TCE (cis-1,2-DCE and trans-1,2-dichloroethylene) were detected at or above the MRLs of 0.02 µg/L in three wells (MW-4S, MW-12S, and MW-9S [estimated]); vinyl chloride was not detected in any groundwater samples above the MRL of 0.1 µg/L.

Figure 13. Altitude of groundwater, direction of groundwater flow, and locations of vertical flow gradients in the (A) shallow and (B) intermediate parts of the shallow aquifer, Capital City Plume Site, Montgomery, Alabama, April–May 2009.

EXPLANATION

Well and identifier

9E● Public supply

MW-7I ● Monitoring—S, shallow; I, intermediate

— *135* — Groundwater contour—Shows altitude of groundwater in shallow aquifer, April–May 2009. Contour intervals 5 and 10 feet. Datum is NGVD 29

157.18 Groundwater altitude—Shows altitude of groundwater in shallow aquifer, April–May 2009. Datum is NGVD 29

↑ ↓ Generalized upward or downward direction of groundwater flow—Between shallow and intermediate parts of shallow aquifer, April–May 2009

⟶ Generalized groundwater-flow direction

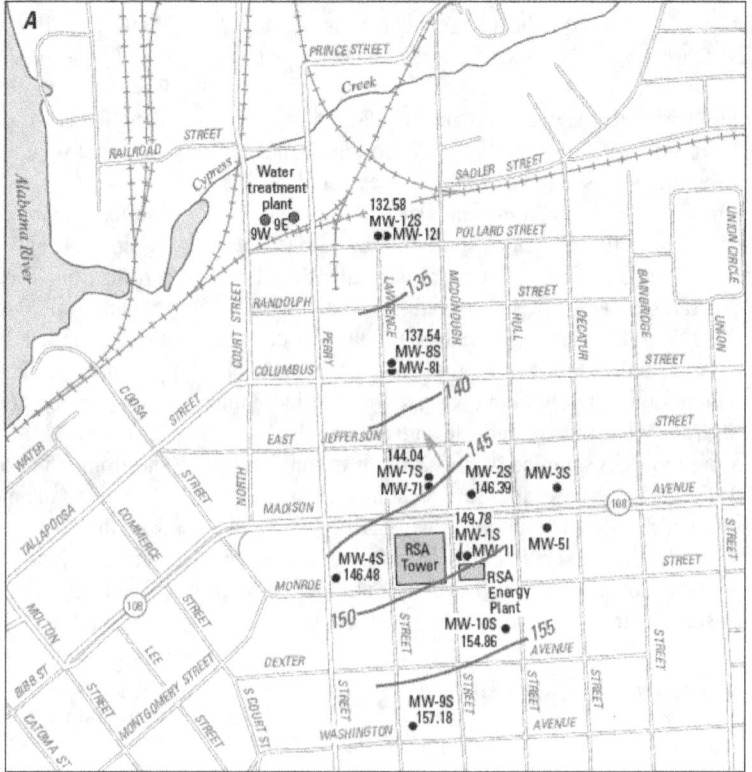

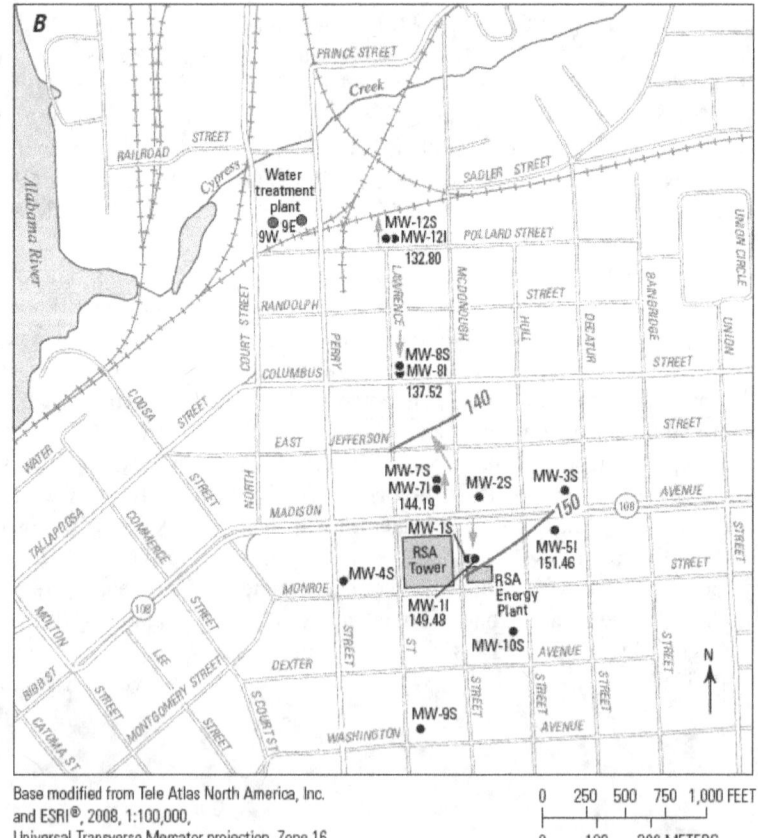

Base modified from Tele Atlas North America, Inc. and ESRI®, 2008, 1:100,000, Universal Transverse Mercator projection, Zone 16

0 250 500 750 1,000 FEET

0 100 200 METERS

Table 4.   Monitoring-well construction data, groundwater altitudes, and field measurements of physical properties and chemical constituents during groundwater-sample collection, Capital City Plume Site, Montgomery, Alabama, April–May 2009.

[TOC, top of casing; NGVD 29, National Geodetic Vertical Datum of 1929; mg/L, milligram per liter; NTU, nephelometric turbidity unit; μS/cm at 25 C, microsiemens per centimeter at 25 degrees Celsius; S, monitoring well in shallow part of shallow aquifer; I, monitoring well in intermediate part of shallow aquifer; nm, not measured]

Well name (fig. 3)	Sample date	Sample time	Well depth	Screened interval	Altitude, TOC (feet above NGVD 29)	Depth to water from TOC (feet)	Altitude of groundwater (feet above NGVD 29)
			(feet below land surface)				
Shallow							
MW-1S	May 19, 2009	11:35	51.96	11.27–21	189.37	39.59	149.78
MW-2S	April 7, 2009	15:00	59.87	40–60	188.59	42.20	146.39
MW-4S	April 21, 2009	9:30	38.75	27–36.7	178.72	32.24	146.48
MW-7S	April 9, 2009	11:15	96.71	84.9–94.6	179.65	35.61	144.04
MW-8S	April 20, 2009	11:40	51.77	40–49.7	173.46	35.92	137.54
MW-9S	April 27, 2009	14:00	71.76	60–69.7	213.41	56.23	157.18
MW-10S	April 27, 2009	10:15	71.91	60.1–69.8	212.67	57.81	154.86
MW-12S	April 23, 2009	11:30	41.88	29.3–38.9	157.58	25.00	132.58
Intermediate							
MW-1I	May 12, 2009	11:30	141.76	130–139.7	190.00	40.52	149.48
MW-5I	April 8, 2009	13:10	159.87	147.6–157.3	210.98	59.52	151.46
MW-7I	April 9, 2009	14:40	128.85	117.1–126.8	179.76	35.57	144.19
MW-8I	April 21, 2009	13:40	119.73	108–117.7	173.42	35.90	137.52
MW-12I	April 22, 2009	12:35	104.69	92.1–101.8	157.82	25.02	132.80

Well name (fig. 3)	Dissolved oxygen[a]	Ferrous iron[a]	Nitrate[a]	Sulfate[a]	Sulfide[a]	Turbidity[a] (NTU)	Temperature[b] (degrees Celsius)	Dissolved oxygen[b] (mg/L)	Specific conductance[b] (μS/cm at 25°C)	pH[b]
	(mg/L)									
Shallow										
MW-1S	5.0	0.01	3.2	7	0	0.43	22.3	5.11	266	7.3
MW-2S	6.3	0.05	6.3	8	0	0.8	21.8	5.9	212	5.2
MW-4S	6.4	0.01	4.5	19	0	1.3	21.5	4.9	322	5.6
MW-7S	4.0	0.04	1.5	4	0	nm	21.8	2.6	70	5.8
MW-8S	5.9	0.01	6.1	9	0	0.5	22.2	6.6	219	5.0
MW-9S	5.5	0.01	1.5	6	0	0.2	22.9	6.0	177	5.1
MW-10S	5.1	0.01	6.4	13	0	0.5	22.6	5.2	249	5.3
MW-12S	5.5	0.02	7.1	5	0	0.1	22.0	4.9	254	5.5
Intermediate										
MW-1I	4.4	0.01	2.9	1	0.01	3.61	20.8	5.55	64	7.7
MW-5I	6.6	0.01	2.2	1	0	0.6	21.7	5.4	60	5.8
MW-7I	6.4	0.01	6.6	6	0	1.7	22.0	6.9	212	5.2
MW-8I	3.6	0.05	1.7	2	0	0.8	21.3	3.35	72	6.0
MW-12I	2.2	0.12	0.7	3	0	0.8	21.2	1.8	91	6.1

[a]Measurements made using a Hach® field kit.

[b]Measurements made using a YSI, Inc., multiparameter probe.

Figure 14. Locations of *(A)* perchloro-ethylene (PCE) and *(B)* trichloroethylene (TCE) detections in groundwater, Capital City Plume Site, Montgomery, Alabama, April–May 2009 (data from the U.S. Geological Survey, except PCE data for well 9W from the Montgomery Water Works and Sanitary Sewer Board).

EXPLANATION

PCE in groundwater *(A)*—
In micrograms per liter, April–May 2009

> 0.03

> 10

> 100

TCE in groundwater *(B)*—
In micrograms per liter, April–May 2009

> 0.02

Well and identifier

9E ● Public supply

MW-7I ● Monitoring—S, shallow; I, intermediate

PDB1 ● Passive diffusion bag (PDB) sampler and identifier, August 2008

○ Tree-core location—See figure 9 for identifier

☐ Former location and years occupied by commercial printing industry

➤ Generalized groundwater-flow direction

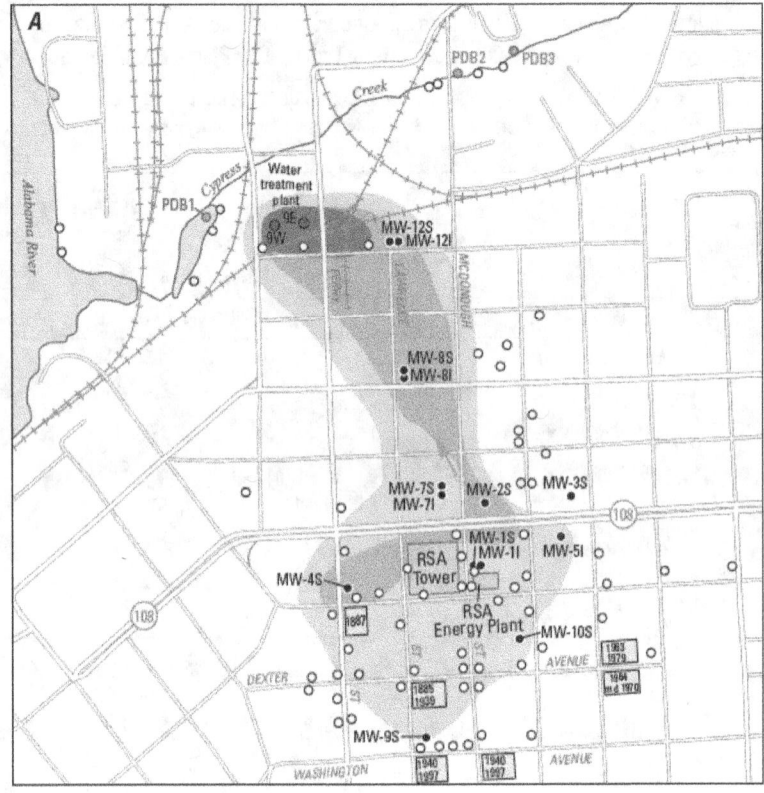

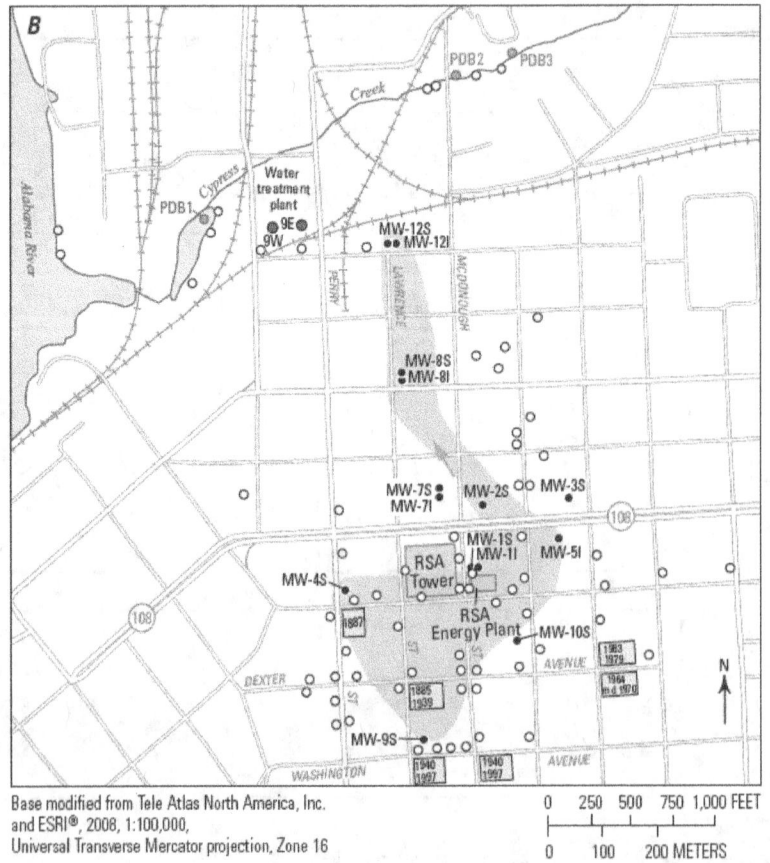

Base modified from Tele Atlas North America, Inc. and ESRI®, 2008, 1:100,000, Universal Transverse Mercator projection, Zone 16

Table 5. Volatile organic compounds in groundwater, Capital City Plume Site, Montgomery, Alabama, April–May 2009.

[µg/L, microgram per liter; MRL, method reporting level; NPDWR, National Primary Drinking Water Regulations (U.S. Environmental Protection Agency, 2009b); MCL, maximum contaminant level; —, no value established; S, identifier for monitoring well in shallow part of shallow aquifer; (E), estimated; <, less than; I, identifier for monitoring well in intermediate part of shallow aquifer]

Well name (fig. 14)	Perchloro-ethylene	Trichloro-ethylene	cis-1,2-dichloro-ethylene	trans-1,2-dichloro-ethylene	Vinyl chloride	1,1-di-chloro-ethylene	1,1,1,2-tetra-chloro-ethane	1,1-di-chloro-ethane	1,2-di-chloro-ethane	Dichloro-methane
					(µg/L)					
MRL	0.04	0.02	0.02	0.02	0.1	0.02	0.04	0.04	0.1	0.04
NPDWR MCL	5	5	70	100	2	—	—	—	—	5
					Shallow					
MW-1S	5.28	0.061(E)	<0.02	0.018(E)	0.08	0.049(E)	<0.04	<0.04	0.06	<0.04
MW-2S	25.0	0.1	<0.02	<0.02	<0.1	0.09(E)	<0.04	<0.04	<0.1	<0.04
MW-4S	84.8	9.62	18.8	0.18	<0.1	<0.02	0.07(E)	<0.04	0.3	<0.04
MW-7S	0.07(E)	0.02	<0.02	<0.02	<0.1	<0.02	<0.04	<0.04	<0.1	<0.04
MW-8S	18.8	0.51	<0.02	<0.02	<0.1	1.68	<0.04	0.04(E)	<0.1	<0.04
MW-9S	0.03(E)	0.03(E)	0.02(E)	<0.02	<0.1	0.13	<0.04	<0.04	<0.1	<0.04
MW-10S	0.07(E)	<0.02	<0.02	<0.02	<0.1	<0.02	<0.04	<0.04	<0.1	<0.04
MW-12S	63.8	0.24	0.18	<0.02	<0.1	<0.02	<0.04	<0.04	<0.1	<0.04
					Intermediate					
MW-1I	0.07(E)	<0.02	<0.02	<0.02	<0.1	<0.02	<0.04	<0.04	<0.1	<0.04
MW-1IR	0.08(E)	<0.02	<0.02	<0.02	<0.1	<0.02	<0.04	<0.04	<0.1	<0.04
MW-5I	7.77	0.51	<0.02	<0.02	<0.1	<0.02	<0.04	<0.04	<0.1	<0.04
MW-7I	0.06(E)	<0.02	<0.02	<0.02	<0.1	<0.02	<0.04	<0.04	<0.1	<0.04
MW-8I	0.01(E)	<0.02	<0.02	<0.02	<0.1	<0.02	<0.04	<0.04	<0.1	<0.04
MW-12I	0.01(E)	0.02(E)	<0.02	<0.02	<0.1	<0.02	<0.04	<0.04	<0.1	<0.04

Well name (fig. 14)	Carbon tetra-chloride	1,2-di-chloro-benzene	Benzene	Toluene	Methyl tert-butyl ether	Diethyl ether	Diiso-propyl ether	1,1,2-tri-chloro-1,2,2-tri-fluoroethane (CFC-113)	Trichloro-fluoro methane (CFC-11)	Chloro-form
					(µg/L)					
MRL	0.06	0.02	0.02	0.02	0.1	0.1	0.06	0.04	0.08	0.04
NPDWR MCL	5	—	5	1,000	—	—	—	—	—	—
					Shallow					
MW-1S	<0.06	<0.02	0.016	0.018	0.15	0.12	<0.06	<0.04	<0.08	37.3
MW-2S	<0.06	<0.02	<0.02	0.03(E)	<0.1	<0.1	<0.06	<0.04	0.06(E)	2.65
MW-4S	<0.06	0.03(E)	0.01(E)	<0.02	<0.1	<0.1	0.22	0.18	0.08(E)	1.96
MW-7S	<0.06	<0.02	<0.02	<0.02	<0.1	<0.1	<0.06	<0.04	<0.08	<0.04
MW-8S	0.18	<0.02	<0.02	<0.02	<0.1	<0.1	<0.06	<0.04	0.25	0.6
MW-9S	<0.06	<0.02	<0.02	<0.02	<0.1	<0.1	<0.06	0.07(E)	0.07(E)	2.98
MW-10S	<0.06	<0.02	<0.02	<0.02	<0.1	<0.1	<0.06	<0.04	<0.08	1.01
MW-12S	<0.06	<0.02	<0.02	0.01(E)	0.7	<0.1	0.22	0.08(E)	<0.08	0.71
					Intermediate					
MW-1I	<0.06	<0.02	<0.02	<0.02	<0.1	<0.1	<0.06	<0.04	<0.08	0.03(E)
MW-1IR	<0.06	<0.02	<0.02	<0.02	<0.1	<0.1	<0.06	<0.04	<0.08	0.04(E)
MW-5I	<0.06	<0.02	<0.02	<0.02	<0.1	<0.1	<0.06	<0.04	<0.08	<0.04
MW-7I	0.18	<0.02	<0.02	<0.02	<0.1	<0.1	<0.06	<0.04	<0.08	1.28
MW-8I	<0.06	<0.02	<0.02	<0.02	<0.1	<0.1	<0.06	<0.04	<0.08	<0.04
MW-12I	<0.06	<0.02	<0.02	<0.02	<0.1	<0.1	<0.06	<0.04	<0.08	<0.04

Additionally, 1,1-dichloroethylene (1,1-DCE) was detected above the MRL in four wells, and the highest concentration (1.68 µg/L) was in well MW-8S (table 5). The solvent 1,1,1,2-tetrachloroethane was detected (estimated) above the MRL of 0.04 µg/L in well MW-4S. The solvent diisopropyl ether was detected above the MRL of 0.06 µg/L in two wells (MW-4S and MW-12S) at a concentration of 0.22 µg/L. 1,2-dichloroethane was detected above the MRL of 0.1 µg/L in well MW-4S. Carbon tetrachloride (CCl_4) was detected in well MW-8S above the MRL of 0.06 µg/L. MTBE was detected above the MRL of 0.1 µg/L in wells MW-1S and MW-12S. Detections of the chlorofluorocarbons CFC-113 and CFC-11 above MRLs of 0.04 and 0.08 µg/L, respectively, occurred in wells MW-4S, MW-9S, and MW-12S for CFC-113, and in wells MW-2S, MW-4S, MW-8S, and MW-9S for CFC-11. Elevated levels of these CFCs in groundwater can be common in urban areas because CFCs were used during many industrial processes (Plummer and Friedman, 1999) prior to the worldwide ban on CFC production implemented in the 2000s. Chloroform was detected in eight wells at concentrations above the MRL of 0.04 µg/L; implications of the detection of CFCs and chloroform for the CCP Site are discussed in a following section.

For the wells screened to the intermediate part of the shallow aquifer, PCE concentrations were measured above the NPDWR MCL in one well (MW-5I) at 7.77 µg/L (table 5). TCE was detected above the MRL also in well MW-5I. CCl_4 was detected in well MW-7I above the MRL of 0.06 µg/L. Chloroform was detected above the MRL of 0.04 µg/L in well MW-7I. Detections of PCE and TCE in the intermediate part of the shallow aquifer imply that contamination detected in the shallow part of the shallow aquifer has been transported to the intermediate part of the shallow aquifer. This PCE and TCE contamination is not a recent phenomenon, because the greater depth of the intermediate wells, compared to the shallower depth of wells in the shallow part of the aquifer (table 4), would require a longer time of contaminant travel.

Comparison of Volatile Organic Compound Detection in Monitoring Wells and Tree Cores

In general, there is good agreement between the occurrence of VOCs detected in groundwater during April–May 2009 (fig. 14) and the occurrence of VOCs detected in tree-cores collected during August 2008 (fig. 15). This agreement is especially evident in the areas where the depth to the water table is no greater than about 35 ft below land surface. This agreement confirms the relation between PCE and TCE detected in tree cores and in groundwater samples collected during July 2007 (Hall, 2007; fig. 10). In general, PCE was detected in trees growing near or upgradient of monitoring wells that contained PCE, such as T12 near well MW-12S, T38 near well MW-4S, and T32 and T31 near well MW-1S.

PCE also was detected in tree cores from areas where no monitoring wells were located, such as T39, but the detections were within the extent of the CCP Site. The highest concentration of PCE in the tree-core vial-headspace was for T32 near the RSA Energy Plant (table 2; fig. 10), where the depth to the water table is about 40 ft below land surface in well MW-1S (table 4). In general, TCE was detected in trees growing near or upgradient of monitoring wells that contained TCE, such as T12 near well MW-12S; T29, T28 and T33 near well MW-1S; and T61 and T64 near well MW-9S (table 4; fig. 10).

The location of the only PDB sampler (PDB1, fig. 15) in Cypress Creek bed sediments near Court Street that had detections of TCE and cis-1,2-DCE and its proximity to the TCE- and PCE-contaminated public-supply wells 9W and 9E indicates that PCE- and TCE-contaminated groundwater discharges to the creek. The detection of cis-1,2-DCE in PDB1 indicates TCE biotransformation under probable anoxic hyporheic zone conditions in Cypress Creek.

Inorganic compounds also were detected in groundwater during April–May 2009 sampling (table 6). Aluminum, iron, and manganese were detected in well MW-12I at 220, 300, and 74.5 µg/L, respectively; all of these values exceed or equal the respective NSDWR MCLs. Chromium was detected in all wells above the MRL; wells screened to the intermediate part of the shallow aquifer had higher chromium concentrations (2.1 to 9.4 µg/L) than wells in the shallow part of the aquifer (1.2 to 6.1 µg/L). Chromium was detected, however, at much lower concentrations than reported for groundwater samples collected during July 2007 (Hall, 2007). A possible explanation for the lower chromium concentrations measured in groundwater samples collected during April–May 2009 is the lower turbidity values relative to the turbidity values reported for the same wells in July 2007 (fig. 16). The lower turbidity values measured by the USGS are a consequence of using low-flow groundwater sampling methods, as previously described.

Chloroform Concentrations in Groundwater

Concentrations of chloroform were low in most wells sampled (0.6 to 0.71 µg/L; table 5). In ambient groundwater in the United States, chloroform is the most frequently detected VOC at a median concentration of 0.08 µg/L (Zogorski and others, 2006). This frequency of detection and low concentration in groundwater is primarily the consequence of the almost century-long and widespread practice of chlorinating drinking-water supplies and wastewater, which has now entered the global hydrologic cycle (Ivahnenko and Zogorski, 2006; Zogorski and others, 2006). Much higher concentrations of chloroform were detected, however, in groundwater from a closely spaced group of shallow wells at the CCP Site—well MW-1S, where the chloroform concentration was 37.3 µg/L, and nearby shallow wells MW-4S, MW-2S, and MW-9S, which had concentrations of 1.96, 2.65, and 2.98 µg/L, respectively (fig. 17).

Figure 15. Locations of a passive diffusion bag (PDB1) sampler on Cypress Creek that had detections of trichloroethylene (TCE) and *cis*-1,2-dichloroethylene (*cis*-1,2-DCE), and trees that had *(A)* perchloroethylene (PCE) and *(B)* TCE detections in tree-core vial headspace, Capital City Plume Site, Montgomery, Alabama, August 2008.

EXPLANATION

PCE in groundwater *(A)*—
Greater than 0.03 micrograms per liter, April–May 2009

PCE detected in vial headspace containing a tree core *(A)*—
In parts per billion by volume (ppbv), August 2008

Above method reporting level (MRL; 2 ppbv)

Greater than 5,000 ppbv

TCE in groundwater *(B)*—
Greater than 0.02 micrograms per liter, April–May 2009

TCE detected in vial headspace containing a tree core *(B)*—
In parts per billion by volume (ppbv), August 2008

Greater than 500 ppbv

Greater than 50,000 ppbv

Well and identifier

9E ● Public supply

MW-7I ● Monitoring—S, shallow; I, intermediate

PDB1 ● Passive diffusion bag sampler and identifier, August 2008

○ Tree-core location—See figure 9 for identifier

Former location and years occupied by commercial printing industry

Generalized groundwater-flow direction

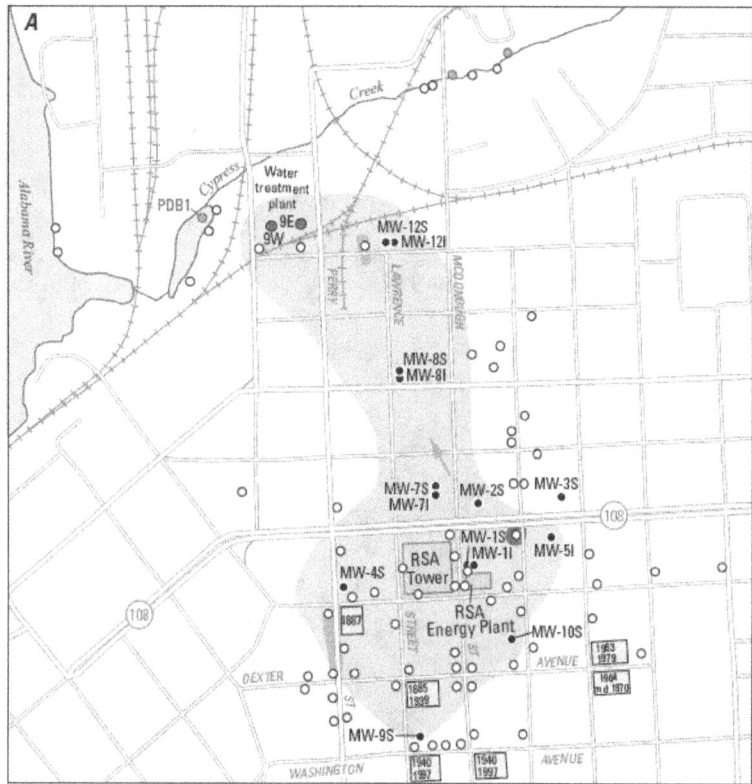

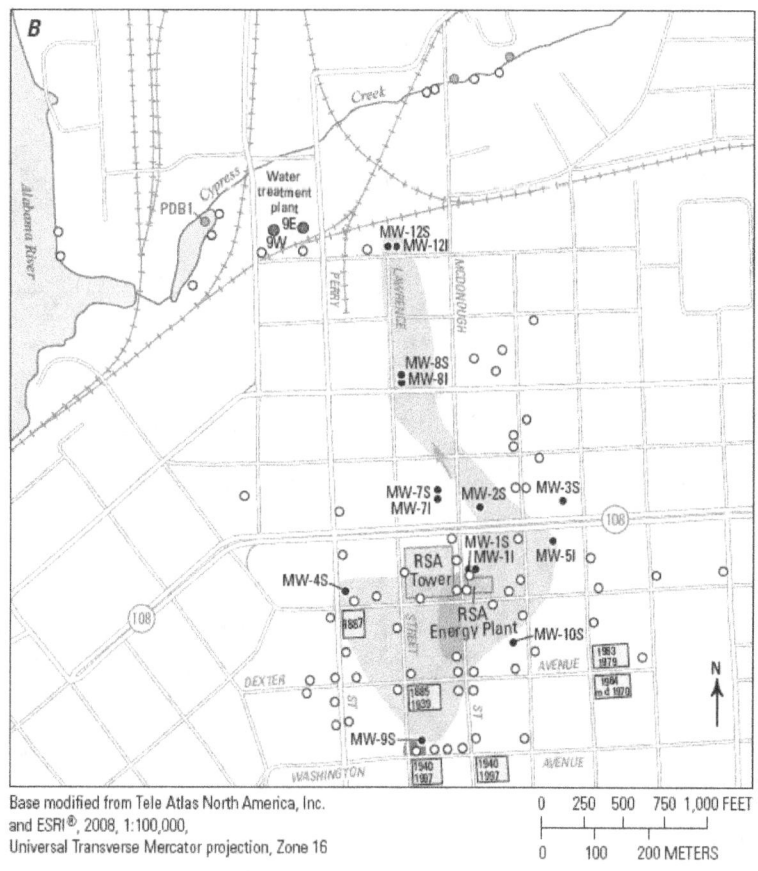

Base modified from Tele Atlas North America, Inc.
and ESRI®, 2008, 1:100,000,
Universal Transverse Mercator projection, Zone 16

0   250   500   750 1,000 FEET

0   100   200 METERS

Table 6. Concentrations of selected inorganic compounds in unfiltered groundwater, Capital City Plume Site, Montgomery, Alabama, April–May 2009.

[µg/L, microgram per liter; mg/L, milligram per liter; MRL, method reporting level; NPDWR, National Primary Drinking Water Regulations (U.S. Environmental Protection Agency, 2009b); MCL, maximum contaminant level; NSDWR, National Secondary Drinking Water Regulations (U.S. Environmental Protection Agency, 2009c); NA, not applicable; —, no value established; (E), estimated; <, less than]

Well name (fig. 3)	Depth of well, feet below land surface	Aluminum	Arsenic	Barium	Beryllium	Cadmium	Calcium	Chromium	Cobalt	Copper	Iron	Lead	Lithium
		(µg/L)					(mg/L)			(µg/L)			
MRL	NA	6	0.2	0.6	0.2	0.06	0.04	0.4	0.1	4	14	0.1	0.08
NPDWR MCL	NA	—	10	200	4	5	—	100	—	1,300	—	15	—
NSDWR MCL	NA	200	—	—	—	—	—	—	—	—	300	—	—
Shallow													
MW-1S	51.96	10.7	0.14(E)	63	<0.2	0.071	11.8	6.1	0.122	2.2(E)	22.2	0.157	1.21
MW-2S	59.87	32	<0.2	69.4	<0.2	0.04(E)	10.5	3.5	<0.1	218	28	1.13	1
MW-4S	38.75	14	<0.2	55.9	0.13(E)	<0.06	7.09	1.2	0.25	101	12(E)	0.18	<0.08
MW-7S	96.71	110	0.2(E)	17.8	<0.2	0.05(E)	3.91	1.4	0.27	<4	75	0.34	2
MW-8S	51.77	9	<0.2	68.1	0.15(E)	0.11	12	3.3	<0.1	40	20	0.91	2
MW-9S	71.76	6.2	<0.2	127	<0.2	0.074	6.57	2.45	<0.1	<4	10.7(E)	0.103	0.91
MW-10S	71.91	8.4	<0.2	56.9	<0.2	0.045(E)	8.73	3.13	.053(E)	15.7	12.2(E)	0.131	0.82
MW-12S	41.88	4	<0.2	106	<0.2	0.13	16.8	3	0.06(E)	50	<14	0.16	2
Intermediate													
MW-1I	141.76	21.7	0.21	34.9	<0.2	0.15	4.38	3.69	0.123	<4	27.9	.077(E)	1.01
MW-5I	159.37	6(E)	<0.2	25.4	<0.2	<0.06	4.26	2.4	<0.1	30	9(E)	0.31	2
MW-7I	128.85	<6	<0.2	133	0.23	<0.06	13.5	5.1	<0.1	98	15	0.45	1
MW-8I	119.73	15	<0.2	35.9	<0.2	<0.06	5.51	9.4	0.24	28	128	0.11	3
MW-12I	104.69	220	0.48	18.9	<0.2	<0.06	6.2	2.1	0.4	14	300	0.13	4

Well name (fig. 3)	Magnesium	Manganese	Mercury	Molybdenum	Nickel	Potassium	Selenium	Silver	Sodium	Strontium	Zinc
	(mg/L)	(µg/L)				(mg/L)	(µg/L)		(mg/L)	(µg/L)	
MRL	0.008	0.4	0.01	0.1	0.2	0.2	0.12	0.06	0.4	0.8	4
NPDWR MCL	—	—	2	—	—	—	50	—	—	—	—
NSDWR MCL	—	50	—	—	—	—	—	100	—	—	500
Shallow											
MW-1S	5.33	6.67	0.009	0.112	9.5	4.21	2.07	<0.06	21	98.8	4.5
MW-2S	4.13	13	0.011	<0.1	3	3.5	2.6	<0.06	18.9	74.4	11
MW-4S	3.3	18.7	<0.01	<0.1	1.1	13	3.3	<0.06	45.1	54	<4
MW-7S	0.512	26.7	<0.01	0.2	4.6	1.74	0.06(E)	<0.06	8.5	87.6	4(E)
MW-8S	3.61	15	<0.01	<0.1	3.5	4.82	1.9	<0.06	18.8	120	6
MW-9S	3.58	7.58	<0.01	<0.1	3.37	2.71	1.69	<0.06	14.9	59.6	3.2(E)
MW-10S	3.76	4.65	<0.01	<0.1	1.73	2.39	3.09	<0.06	25.6	47.7	2.9(E)
MW-12S	4.34	1.8	<0.01	<0.1	4.6	4.34	2.1	<0.06	18.5	118	12
Intermediate											
MW-1I	0.415	3.97	<0.01	0.186	8.1	1.53	0.09(E)	<0.06	4.98	61.8	<4
MW-5I	0.58	0.9	<0.01	<0.1	0.61	2.04	<0.12	<0.06	4.8	73.7	<4
MW-7I	2.71	2.7	<0.01	<0.1	2.3	3.2	5.6	<0.06	16.2	146	9
MW-8I	0.61	6.8	<0.01	<0.1	18.5	1.78	0.09(E)	<0.06	6.2	97.1	<4
MW-12I	0.795	74.5	<0.01	0.7	2.9	2.08	0.22	<0.06	11	127	<4

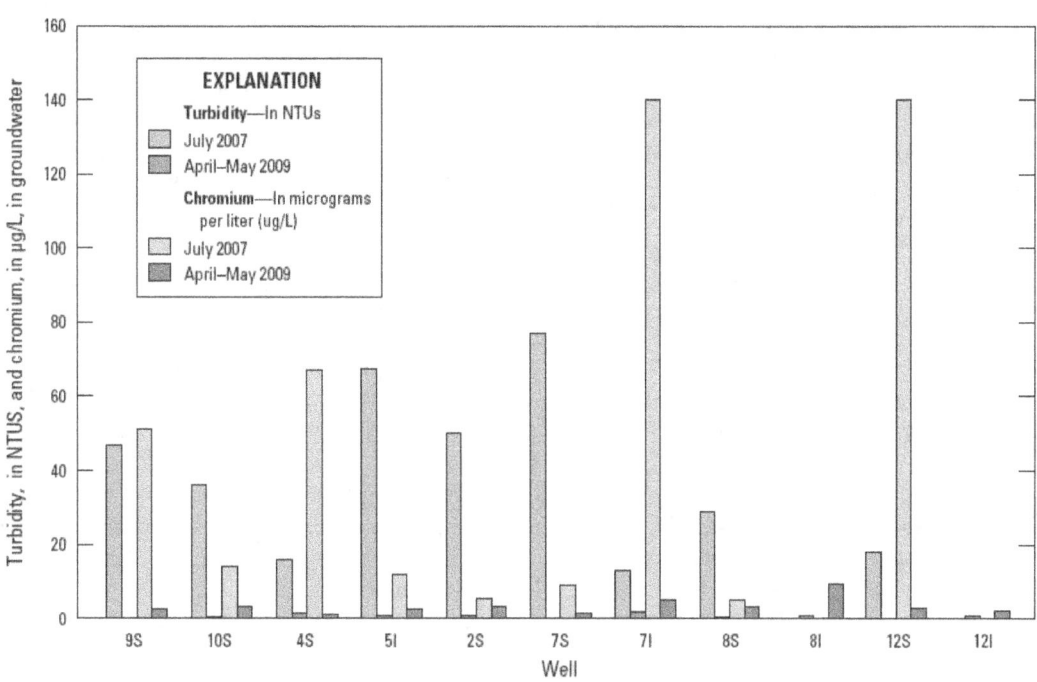

Figure 16. Relation of turbidity values and total chromium concentrations in groundwater samples collect d   007 and during April–May 2009, Capital City Plume Site, Montgomery, Alabam .

Figure 17. Locations of wells with chloroform concentrations greater than 1 microgram per liter, Capital City Plume Site, Montgomery, Alabama, April–May 2009.

EXPLANATION

Chloroform in groundwater—
In micrograms per liter,
April–May 2009

  > 1

> 35

Well and identifier
Public supply

Monitoring—S, shallow;
I, intermediate

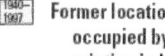 **Former location and years occupied by commercial printing industry**

Generalized groundwater-flow direction

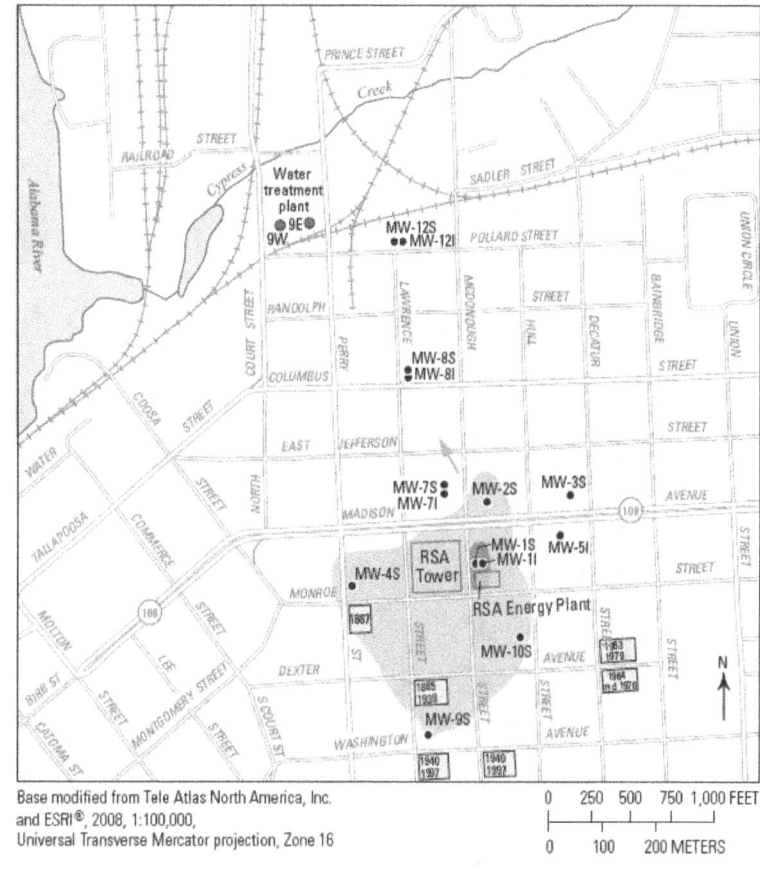

Base modified from Tele Atlas North America, Inc.
and ESRI®, 2008, 1:100,000,
Universal Transverse Mercator projection, Zone 16

Chloroform in groundwater at concentrations greater than ambient local and regional levels indicates recharge from treated municipal water in addition to water supplied by ambient precipitation (Ivahnenko and Barbash, 2004). Minear and Amy (1996) reported that chloroform concentrations typically range from 2 to 44 µg/L in chlorinated drinking water. Municipal water chlorinated by the MWWSSB during 2010 had concentrations of total trihalomethanes, of which chloroform is the primary component, ranging from 27 to 36 µg/L (Montgomery Water Works and Sanitary Sewer Board, 2010). Additional evidence of localized recharge by treated municipal water in the vicinity of well MW-1S is the measured pH of 7.3 in that well relative to the mean pH of 5.35 for the other shallow wells (table 4). The pH of treated water delivered by the MWWSSB ranged from 7.8 to 9.3 in 2010 (Montgomery Water Works and Sanitary Sewer Board, 2010). Moreover, the measured pH of 7.7 in the deeper well (MW-1I) at the same location indicates that municipal water has migrated to the intermediate part of the shallow aquifer, as would be indicated by the downward vertical head gradient at that location (fig. 13*B*).

The presence of chemicals and properties associated with treated municipal water, such as chloroform and high pH, in the shallow and intermediate parts of the shallow aquifer indicates the presence of treated municipal water at depths at least 30 ft below land surface if not greater. Conversely,

the absence of chloroform and high pH in other wells in the shallow part of the shallow aquifer at the CCP Site raises the question: "How did treated municipal water recharge shallow groundwater, and why only in this limited area?" The simplest explanation is that the treated municipal water, following use and disposal, has reached shallow groundwater by migrating through potential cracks, joints, or decreased gradients in the pipes or junction boxes of the City of Montgomery's sanitary sewer system, or in areas where the sewer system may be inadvertently connected to the stormwater system. In fact, the steepest gradients between sewer outfalls in the CCP Site occur between Washington and Dexter Avenues, where gradients between junction boxes are 16.8 to 21.3 percent (fig. 18; data from the Montgomery Water Works and Sanitary Sewer Board, illustration by the U.S. Geological Survey). Sewer systems have been documented at other sites to provide a pathway for the migration of subsurface contamination (Vroblesky, Petkewich, and others, 2009). However, the delineation of potential cracks was beyond the scope of this investigation, and would require the use of sewer and pipe video inspection equipment.

The zone of shallow wells characterized by high chloroform concentrations during groundwater sampling in April–May 2009 also contain groundwater characterized by PCE and TCE contamination. This co-occurrence of treated municipal water in wells that also contain PCE and TCE

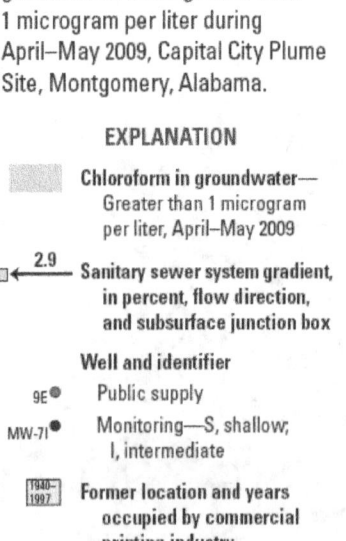

Figure 18. Approximate locations of the sanitary sewer system and slopes between sewer junction boxes with presumed flow directions in relation to the area where chloroform concentrations in groundwater were greater than 1 microgram per liter during April–May 2009, Capital City Plume Site, Montgomery, Alabama.

EXPLANATION

Chloroform in groundwater—
Greater than 1 microgram per liter, April–May 2009

2.9 ⊡◄— Sanitary sewer system gradient, in percent, flow direction, and subsurface junction box

Well and identifier

9E● Public supply

MW-7I● Monitoring—S, shallow; I, intermediate

Former location and years occupied by commercial printing industry

Generalized groundwater-flow direction

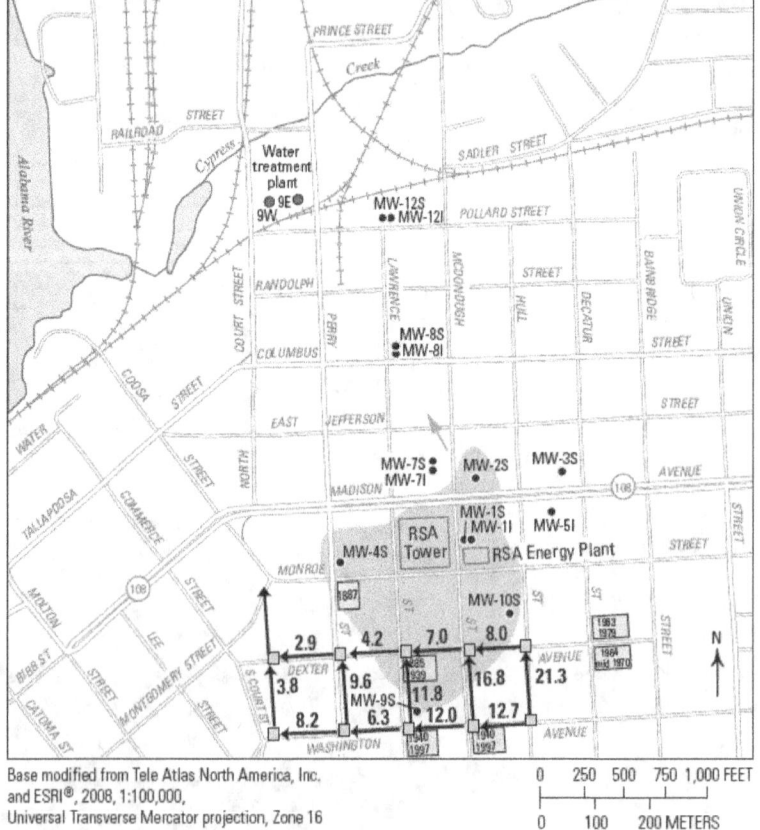

Base modified from Tele Atlas North America, Inc. and ESRI®, 2008, 1:100,000, Universal Transverse Mercator projection, Zone 16

provides geochemical evidence as to how the groundwater beneath the RSA Energy Plant, where no contaminant source had been found, could have become contaminated. The proposed pathway revealed by this co-occurrence of chloroform, PCE, and TCE contamination is that industrial wastewater containing PCE and TCE entered the sanitary sewer system upgradient from the RSA Energy Plant, leaked from the sanitary sewer system (and from the stormwater system in areas where connections to the sewer system remain) into the subsurface, and then migrated through the unsaturated zone to recharge groundwater near well MW-1S. Specifically, industrial wastewater from commercial printing industries located along Washington and Dexter Avenues was disposed of down sink drains, floor drains, and sumps (U.S. Environmental Protection Agency, 2009a) and was mixed over time with municipal wastewater from the same locations. The wastewater then would have flowed downgradient and entered the subsurface through leaks to recharge the water table beneath the RSA Energy Plant, following infiltration through the 30- to 50-ft-thick unsaturated zone. This proposed contamination pathway also may explain why no near-surface soil contamination by PCE or TCE has been detected near the RSA Energy Plant during previous investigations since 1993. This proposed pathway of contamination also is supported by the fact that the acute exposure of workers to vapors occurred near the RSA Energy Plant only after the excavation reached depths near the water table, rather than near land surface.

Investigation of the Probable Release History

To further investigate the occurrence of the past disposal of industrial wastewater that contained PCE and TCE into the sanitary sewer and (or) stormwater systems at the CCP Site, concentrations of SF_6 and CFCs in groundwater samples were measured. In addition, because trees can interact with sources of water located above the water table, dendrochemistry was used to provide a range of potential dates when particular trees had been exposed to chlorinated solvents released to the subsurface.

Sulfur Hexafluoride and Chlorofluorocarbon Concentrations and Estimated Recharge Dates

Groundwater in the shallow aquifer characterized by the highest chloroform concentrations during April–May 2009 also was characterized by the youngest (most recent) ground-water recharge dates, from about 1994 to 2008, as determined from SF_6 concentrations and using the piston-type ground-water-flow model (table 7; fig. 19). Conversely, groundwater characterized by the lowest chloroform concentrations also was characterized by the lowest SF_6 concentrations, indicating the presence of water recharged prior to about 1992. The

younger recharge dates confirm the presence of recently recharged water in the area centered around wells MW-1S and MW-2S, relative to groundwater with older recharge age dates (from about 1958 to 1992) in the surrounding wells. The presence of younger recharge in shallow groundwater in this area confirms the existence of hydraulic connection between land surface and groundwater, as was implied by the detection of PCE and TCE in these wells. Moreover, the recent recharge dates indicate the hydraulic connection still exists. Groundwater samples collected from the intermediate part of the shallow aquifer during April–May 2009 where chloroform was not detected, was characterized by recharge that occurred between about 1952 and 1970.

Groundwater from all wells sampled in the shallow and intermediate parts of the shallow aquifer during May 2010 was characterized by concentrations of CFCs measured in picograms per kilogram (pg/kg; table 8; 1 pg = 1.0×10^{-9} milligrams). The detection of CFCs in groundwater in wells MW-1S, MW-2S, MW-4S, MW-8S, MW-9S, MW-10S, MW12S, and MW-7I at concentrations greater than ambient atmospheric levels in equilibrium with water indicates contamination by input from local industrial sources of CFCs, including the use of CFCs as a solvent by the commercial printing industry. Five of the seven CFC-contaminated shallow wells (MW-1S, MW-2S, MW-4S, MW-9S, and MW-10S) and the only CFC-contaminated intermediate well (MW-7I) also had elevated concentrations of chloroform and CFCs during April–May 2009 (table 5).

One well in the shallow part and four wells in the inter-mediate part of the shallow aquifer characterized by ambient atmospheric CFC concentrations were used to determine the recharge date of groundwater, assuming a piston-type groundwater-flow model. Two groundwater samples from well MW-7S were used to determine CFC-based recharge dates in the late 1940s—the oldest recharge date of all shallow wells sampled. This recharge date is confirmed by the presence of low SF_6 concentrations, which also indicated the oldest recharge dates (between about 1952 and 1964) of all shallow wells sampled. Groundwater sampled from the intermediate wells had recharge dates from the mid-1940s to the early 1960s. The oldest recharge date (mid-1940s) was for the most downgradient well sampled, well MW-12I. An upgradient well (MW-7S) had a CFC-based recharge date of about 1948, and well MW-1I farther upgradient had the youngest CFC-based recharge date of about 1960 (table 8; fig. 20). The wells with recent recharge dates coincide with wells that had detections of chloroform in groundwater samples. The wells in the shallow part of the shallow aquifer characterized by groundwater with more recent recharge dates determined from SF_6 concentrations (average of about 1991) were characterized by the highest CFC concentrations. Wells in the intermediate part of the shallow aquifer characterized by groundwater with the oldest recharge dates determined from SF_6 concentrations (average of about 1958) tended to be characterized by the lowest CFC concentrations.

Table 7. Concentrations of sulfur hexafluoride (SF_6) in shallow and intermediate groundwater, Capital City Plume Site, Montgomery, Alabama, May 2010.

[cm^3, cubic centimeter; Mol/kg, moles per kilogram; recharge age and date assume piston-type groundwater flow; S, identifier for monitoring well in shallow part of shallow aquifer; I, identifier for monitoring well in intermediate part of shallow aquifer]

Well (fig. 19)	Date collected	Time collected	Sample bottle headspace (cm^3)	SF_6 concentration, in groundwater (Mol/kg)	Model SF_6 recharge age (years before 2010)	Model SF_6 recharge date (approximate)
Shallow						
MW-1S	May 19, 2010	1405	0.00	1.67	6.9	2003
MW-1S	May 19, 2010	1405	0.00	1.71	6.4	2004
MW-2S	May 24, 2010	1130	0.20	1.65	1.4	2009
MW-2S	May 24, 2010	1130	0.40	1.59	2.4	2008
MW-4S	May 18, 2010	1415	0.16	1.2	13.4	1997
MW-4S	May 18, 2010	1415	0.16	1.44	9.9	2000
MW-7S	May 19, 2010	1015	0.40	0.05	46.4	1964
MW-7S	May 19, 2010	1015	0.14	0.02	58.4	1952
MW-8S	May 17, 2010	1400	0.60	0.68	22.9	1988
MW-8S	May 17, 2010	1400	0.14	0.71	22.4	1988
MW-9S	May 25, 2010	1315	0.12	0.71	21.9	1986
MW-9S	May 25, 2010	1315	0.20	0.68	22.4	1988
MW-10S	May 25, 2010	945	1.30	1.06	15.9	1995
MW-10S	May 25, 2010	945	1.30	1.07	15.9	1995
MW-12S	May 12, 2010	1415	0.14	1.05	17.9	1993
MW-12S	May 12, 2010	1415	0.80	1.04	18.4	1992
Intermediate						
MW-1I	May 19, 2010	1400	1.10	0.02	58.4	1952
MW-1I	May 19, 2010	1400	0.40	0.02	58.4	1952
MW-5I	May 24, 2010	1500	0.00	0.03	58.4	1952
MW-5I	May 24, 2010	1500	0.00	0.04	49.4	1961
MW-7I	May 19, 2010	930	0.10	0.11	38.9	1972
MW-7I	May 19, 2010	930	0.00	0.1	40.4	1970
MW-8I	May 13, 2010	1125	0.12	0.03	58.4	1952
MW-8I	May 13, 2010	1125	0.00	0.03	56.9	1953
MW-12I	May 12, 2010	1100	0.12	0.05	47.9	1963
MW-12I	May 12, 2010	1100	0.40	0.03	51.9	1959
Dionized water, aerated						
	June 17, 2010	607	0.00	1.65	0.5	2010
	June 18, 2010	538	0.00	1.59	1.5	2009

Figure 19. Groundwater recharge dates estimated from sulfur hexafluoride (SF$_6$) concentrations in monitoring wells in the shallow and intermediate parts of the shallow aquifer, Capital City Plume Site, Montgomery, Alabama, May 2010.

EXPLANATION

 **Chloroform in groundwater—** Greater than 1 microgram per liter, April–May 2009

Groundwater recharge date, based on SF$_6$ concentration, May 2010

2003   Shallow well

1952   Intermediate well

Well and identifier

9E ⊙   Public supply

MW-7I ●   Monitoring—S, shallow; I, intermediate

[1940–1997]   Former location and years occupied by commercial printing industry

→   Generalized groundwater-flow direction

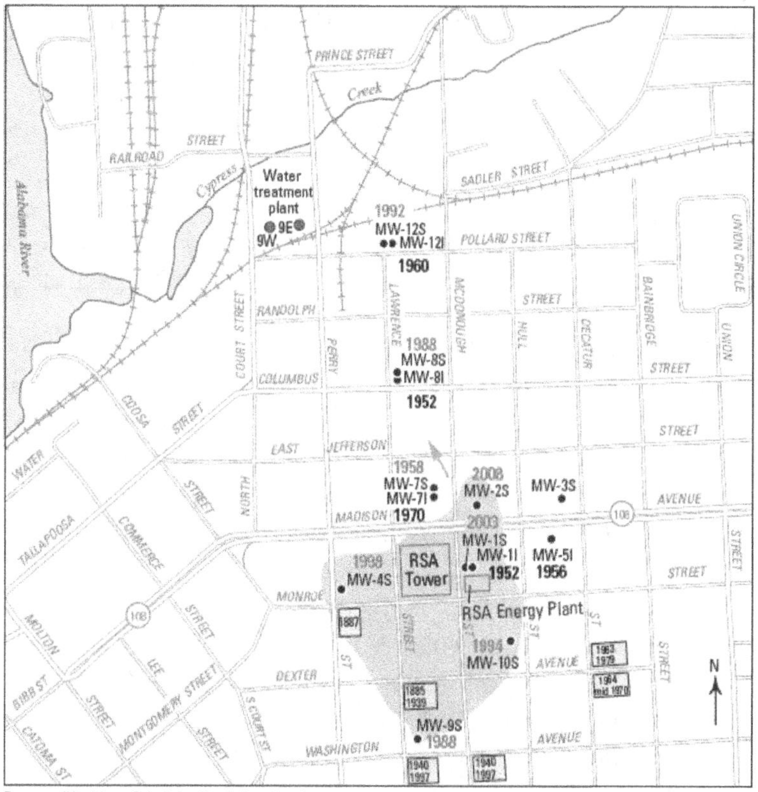

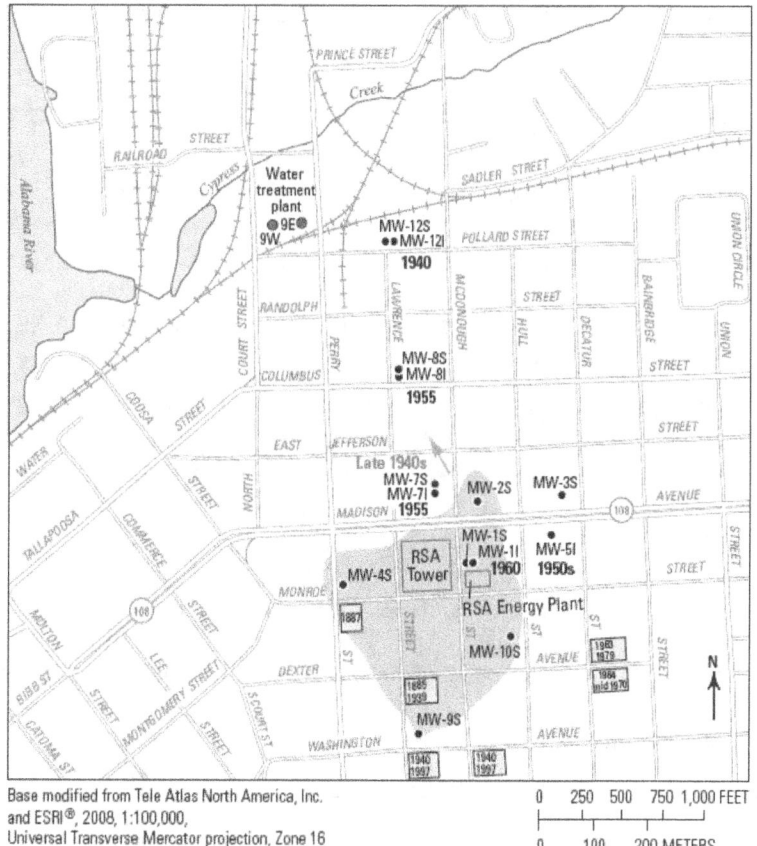

Base modified from Tele Atlas North America, Inc. and ESRI®, 2008, 1:100,000, Universal Transverse Mercator projection, Zone 16

Figure 20. Groundwater recharge dates estimated from chlorofluoro-carbon (CFC) concentrations in groundwater, Capital City Plume Site, Montgomery, Alabama, May 2010.

EXPLANATION

Chloroform in groundwater— Greater than 1 microgram per liter, April–May 2009

Groundwater recharge date, based on CFC concentration, May 2010

Late 1940s   Shallow well

1955   Intermediate well

Well and identifier

9E ⊙   Public supply

MW-7I ●   Monitoring—S, shallow; I, intermediate

[1940–1997]   Former location and years occupied by commercial printing industry

→   Generalized groundwater-flow direction

Base modified from Tele Atlas North America, Inc. and ESRI®, 2008, 1:100,000, Universal Transverse Mercator projection, Zone 16

Table 8.   Chlorofluorocarbon concentrations in groundwater and estimated recharge dates, Capital City Site, Montgomery, Alabama, May 2010.

[pg/kg, picogram per kilogram; CFC, chlorofluorocarbon; S, identifier for monitoring well in shallow part of shallow aquifer; I, identifier for monitoring well in intermediate part of shallow aquifer; Con., contaminated by excess CFC from a non-atmospheric source; five samples were collected at each well; the sample results are for samples selected by the laboratory for analysis; —, no date could be estimated because of contamination]

Well	Date collected	Time collected	Concentration (pg/kg)			Piston-type flow ages, years before 2010			Estimated recharge date
			CFC-11	CFC-12	CFC-113	CFC-11	CFC-12	CFC-113	
Shallow									
MW-1S	May 19, 2010	1405	7.13E+03	6.69E+04	2.58E+02	Con.	Con.	Con.	—
MW-1S	May 19, 2010	1405	7.23E+03	5.16E+04	2.41E+02	Con.	Con.	Con.	—
MW-1S	May 19, 2010	1405	7.00E+03	6.88E+04	2.53E+02	Con.	Con.	Con.	—
MW-2S	May 24, 2010	1130	1.06E+04	8.19E+03	1.53E+02	Con.	Con.	Con.	—
MW-2S	May 24, 2010	1130	1.05E+04	7.85E+03	1.58E+02	Con.	Con.	Con.	—
MW-4S	May 18, 2010	1415	9.76E+03	5.00E+03	1.34E+06	Con.	Con.	Con.	—
MW-4S	May 18, 2010	1415	1.24E+04	4.89E+03	1.39E+06	Con.	Con.	Con.	—
MW-7S	May 19, 2010	1015	1.20E+01	3.63E+00	0.00E+00	54.4	61.4	57.4	Late 1940s
MW-7S	May 19, 2010	1015	9.48E+00	2.90E+00	0.00E+00	55.4	61.9	57.4	Late 1940s
MW-8S	May 13, 2010	1400	1.41E+04	3.32E+05	8.46E+02	Con.	Con.	Con.	—
MW-8S	May 13, 2010	1400	1.45E+04	3.16E+05	9.11E+02	Con.	Con.	Con.	—
MW-9S	May 25, 2010	1315	1.26E+04	1.16E+04	1.19E+06	Con.	Con.	Con.	—
MW-9S	May 25, 2010	1315	1.26E+04	1.22E+04	1.29E+06	Con.	Con.	Con.	—
MW-10S	May 25, 2010	945	7.14E+03	3.72E+03	1.34E+02	Con.	Con.	Con.	—
MW-10S	May 25, 2010	945	8.03E+03	3.73E+03	1.27E+02	Con.	Con.	Con.	—
MW-12S	May 12, 2010	1415	1.40E+04	2.19E+04	1.64E+06	Con.	Con.	Con.	—
MW-12S	May 12, 2010	1415	1.40E+04	2.24E+04	1.66E+06	Con.	Con.	Con.	—
Intermediate									
MW-1I	May 19, 2010	1400	3.57E+01	2.21E+01	2.81E+00	48.4	49.4	45.4	Late 1950s to early 1960s
MW-1I	May 19, 2010	1400	2.23E+01	1.62E+01	4.12E+00	50.9	51.9	42.9	Late 1950s to early 1960s
MW-1I	May 19, 2010	1400	1.64E+01	1.22E+01	2.44E+00	52.9	53.9	46.9	Late 1950s to early 1960s
MW-5I	May 24, 2010	1500	3.74E+01	1.45E+01	8.06E+00	48.4	52.9	38.4	Mid-1950s
MW-5I	May 24, 2010	1500	3.50E+01	1.20E+01	8.99E+00	48.9	54.4	37.4	Mid-1950s
MW-7I	May 19, 2010	930	8.75E+02	1.17E+03	5.77E+02	Con.	Con.	Con.	—
MW-7I	May 19, 2010	930	8.43E+02	1.23E+03	5.15E+02	Con.	Con.	Con.	—
MW-8I	May 13, 2010	1125	6.83E+01	0.00E+00	2.25E+00	44.9	Con.	47.4	Mid- to late 1950s
MW-8I	May 13, 2010	1125	1.34E+02	1.72E+01	2.44E+00	40.9	51.9	46.9	Mid- to late 1950s
MW-8I	May 13, 2010	1125	5.22E+01	1.10E+01	1.87E+00	46.4	54.9	48.9	Mid- to late 1950s
MW-8I	May 13, 2010	1125	6.14E+01	1.62E+01	2.44E+00	45.9	51.9	46.9	Mid- to late 1950s
MW-12I	May 12, 2010	1100	9.89E+00	1.93E+00	0.00E+00	54.9	63.4	57.4	Mid-1940s
MW-12I	May 12, 2010	1100	7.83E+00	2.18E+00	0.00E+00	55.9	62.9	57.4	Mid-1940s

The age difference between groundwater from well MW-11 (about 1960) and downgradient well MW-12I (about mid-1940s) relative to the distance between these wells (about 1,900 ft) indicates an estimated groundwater-flow rate of about 95 ft/yr. This flow rate from estimated recharge age dates is in good agreement with the rate of 100 ft/yr determined using hydrologic properties of the shallow aquifer (Black & Veatch, 2002).

The well with the longest period of record for PCE and TCE concentrations in groundwater is public-supply well 9W, which can be used to shed light on the history of chlorinated-solvent transport and release at the CCP Site. PCE was detected in April 1991 at 7.1 µg/L in a groundwater sample from well 9W (fig. 21); the presence of TCE is unknown, as it was either analyzed and not reported or was not analyzed at that time. A concentration of TCE was detected at 0.57 µg/L during July 2000, however, and the TCE concentration increased to a peak of 2.69 µg/L during April 2003; thereafter, the concentration began to decrease steadily to 0.71 µg/L during April 2009. The PCE concentration in well 9W increased since April 1991 to a high of 58.1 µg/L during July 1997 before beginning to decrease at about the time that nearby well 9E (located just east of well 9W, fig. 3) was turned off in 1997 because of PCE contamination. Since 2002, PCE concentrations have risen in well 9W to 161 µg/L in April 2009.

Possible explanations for the detection of PCE before TCE in well 9W and the trends in these contaminants over time may be related to differences in the location of potential source areas, contaminant release times, physicochemical properties, or sample collection times. For example, PCE may have been used and released prior to the use and release of TCE within the CCP Site and, therefore, was initially detected before TCE in well 9W. On the other hand, TCE is five times more soluble in water than is PCE (about 1,100 mg/L for TCE compared to 200 mg/L for PCE at 20 degrees Celsius). As a result of this solubility difference, PCE and TCE released at the same location at the same time would result in TCE concentrations being detected first in a well downgradient of a release area. The time-series trend in PCE and TCE concentrations in groundwater samples from well 9W (fig. 21) indicate the initial arrival of a maximum concentration of TCE prior to a maximum concentration of PCE—it remains unclear, however, if the high concentration of PCE measured during April 2009 (161 µg/L) is the maximum PCE concentration.

The measured peak TCE concentration in groundwater from well 9W during April 2003, when combined with the estimated groundwater-flow rate, can be used to estimate the time when TCE was released from potential source areas. In this example, TCE concentrations are considered

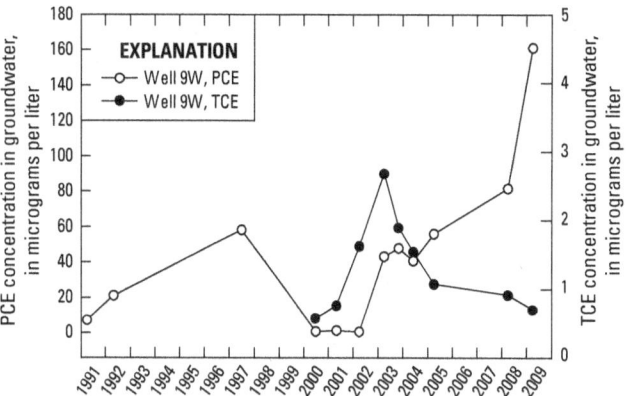

Figure 21. Trends in perchloroethylene (PCE) and trichloroethylene (TCE) concentrations in well 9W, pital Cit   me   e   on g m ry, A   b ma
–

to behave conservatively and transported at rates near those of groundwater flow at the CCP Site, as the shallow aquifer is oxic and, therefore, precludes losses in TCE concentrations as a result of reductive dechlorination. This example also assumes that the TCE is already in the shallow aquifer, and additional time would be necessary to account for the transport of water that contained TCE through the unsaturated zone. The distance between well 9W and the location of a potential source area upgradient near well MW-9S is about 3,000 ft. At a groundwater-flow rate of about 100 ft/yr, to explain the peak TCE concentration measured in well 9W in 2003, a release of TCE near well MW-9S would have occurred about 30 yrs before, in the early 1970s. This falls within the time period between 1940 and 1997 when a commercial printing industry operated upgradient of well MW-9S along Washington Avenue (fig. 14).

The trend in PCE and TCE concentrations measured in well 9W since April 1991 also can be compared to the trend in PCE and TCE concentrations (when available) in monitoring wells located upgradient of well 9W. In well MW-2S, the PCE concentration decreased from 113 µg/L during October 1993 to 25 µg/L during April 2009 (table 5; fig. 22A). Conversely, PCE concentrations in downgradient well 9W during the same period increased from 21 to 161 µg/L. Because the elapsed time between the highest measured PCE concentrations in wells MW-2S and 9W is about 16 yrs (1993 to 2009), and the distance between these two wells is roughly 2,100 ft, a maximum contaminant transport rate for PCE between the two wells would be about 131 ft/yr, slightly higher than that of the groundwater-flow rate previously calculated for the shallow aquifer at the CCP Site.

The average PCE concentration measured in wells MW-3S and 9W was about 27 µg/L until July 2000 when PCE concentrations in well 9W decreased to 0.72 µg/L; in January 2001, PCE in well MW-3S increased slightly to 22 µg/L (fig. 22*B*). In April 2003, PCE concentrations increased in both wells, although to a greater extent in 9W. For TCE, the concentration in well MW-3S decreased from 18 µg/L in May 2000 to 7.8 µg/L in July 2007; meanwhile, the concentration of TCE in well 9W never exceeded 2.69 µg/L. In well MW-4S between January 2001 and April 2009, the concentration of PCE was between 5 and 12 times greater than the concentration of TCE (fig. 22*C*); this scenario of relatively high and stable PCE concentrations may reflect the occurrence

of residual PCE in the unsaturated zone or continued supply from upgradient residual source areas. Concentrations of PCE in well MW-8S decreased from 85 µg/L during May 2000 to 18.8 µg/L during April 2009 (table 5; fig. 22*D*), whereas the concentration of PCE increased considerably in downgradient well 9W during this same period. Concentrations of PCE in well MW-12S decreased from 300 µg/L during July 2007 to 63.8 µg/L during April 2009 (table 5; fig. 22*E*), whereas the PCE concentration increase in well 9W to 161 µg/L. Essentially, the time-series trend in concentrations of PCE and, to a lesser extent TCE, in wells 9W, MW-2S, MW-3S, MW-4S, and MW-8S records the transport of PCE and TCE in groundwater from upgradient potential source areas.

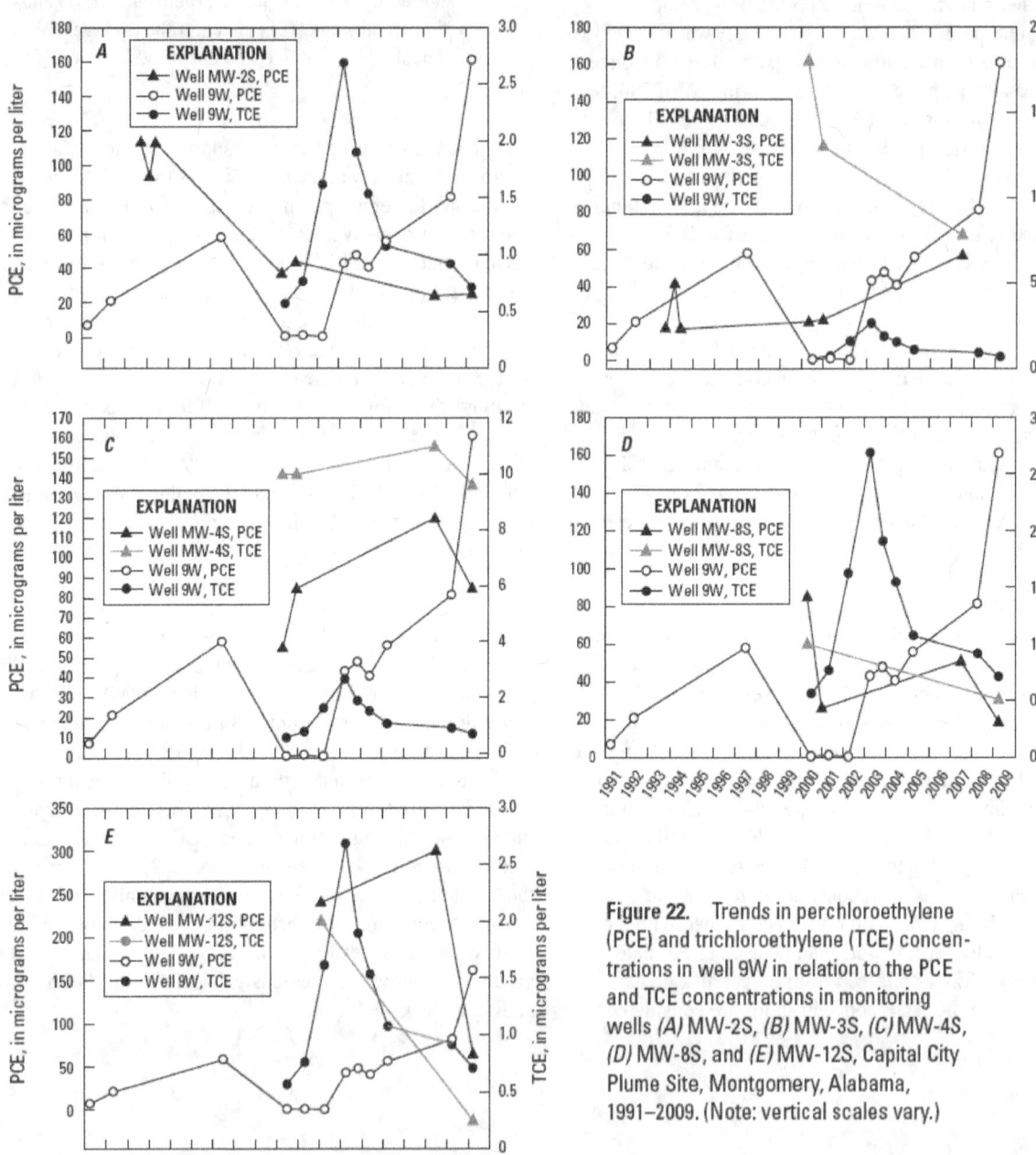

Figure 22. Trends in perchloroethylene (PCE) and trichloroethylene (TCE) concentrations in well 9W in relation to the PCE and TCE concentrations in monitoring wells *(A)* MW-2S, *(B)* MW-3S, *(C)* MW-4S, *(D)* MW-8S, and *(E)* MW-12S, Capital City Plume Site, Montgomery, Alabama, 1991–2009. (Note: vertical scales vary.)

Dendrochemistry

A subset of trees either characterized by detections of chlorinated solvents or growing adjacent to wells that contained PCE- and TCE-contaminated groundwater during the August 2008 tree-core survey (fig. 10) and also contained chloride detections that exceeded the mean value for all trees cored (fig. 12) were re-cored during January 2009 (fig. 23). The concentrations of chloride in core samples from representative trees T47 and T23 were measured in the annual rings that represent tree growth from the late 1940s to January 2009. The highest chloride concentration (94.7 ppm) detected in tree T47 occurred in annual rings formed in the late 1960s; the highest chloride concentration (183.8 ppm) detected in tree T23 occurred in annual rings formed in the mid 1970s. Although no monitoring wells were present at these locations during this time interval, the time period of highest chloride concentration in these trees corroborates the probable release history during the late 1960s and mid-1970s shown previously using trends in PCE and TCE concentrations measured in downgradient well 9W. Moreover, evidence of a potential earlier release is indicated by the high concentration of chloride detected in annual rings of tree T47 formed prior to the late 1960s (fig. 24).

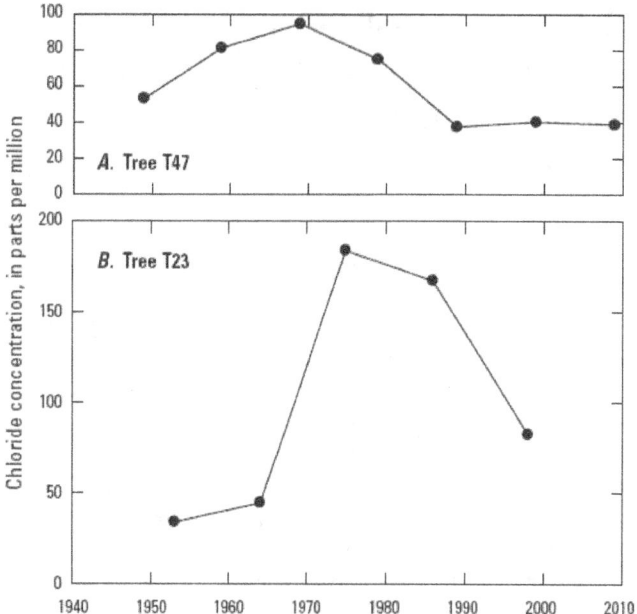

Fig re 24. Concentrations of chloride in annual r gs of core samples from trees *(A)* T47 and *(B)* T23 growing above groundwater contaminated with perchloroethylene (PCE) and trichloroethylene (TCE), Capital City Plume Site, Montgomery, Alabama, 1950–2009.

Figure 23. Locations of trees cored for dendrochemistry analysis, Capital City Plume Site, Montgomery, Alabama, January 2009.

EXPLANATION

○ Tree re-cored during January 2009 for dendrochemistry

○ Results for specific trees shown in figure 24

Well and identifier

9E ● Public supply

MW-7I ● Monitoring—S, shallow; I, intermediate

▢ 1940–1997 Former location and years occupied by commercial printing industry

➤ Generalized groundwater-flow direction

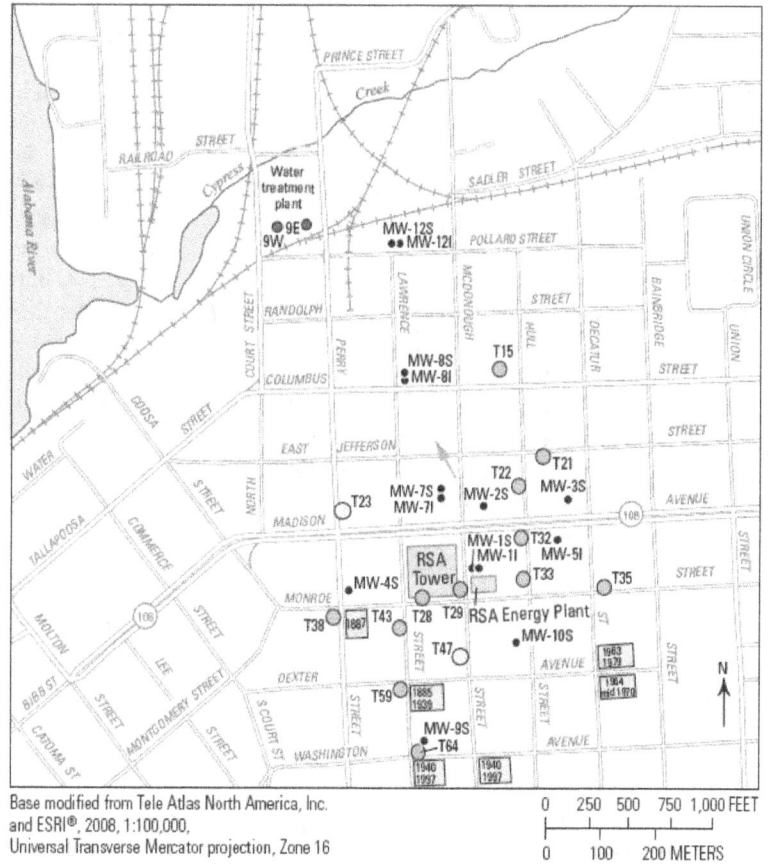

Base modified from Tele Atlas North America, Inc. and ESRI®, 2008, 1:100,000, Universal Transverse Mercator projection, Zone 16

Relation of Commercial Printing and Chlorinated Solvents in Contaminated Groundwater at the Capital City Plume Site

Commercial printing is one of the largest industries in the United States (Printers' National Environmental Assistance Center, 2011). The commercial printing industry uses large volumes of organic and inorganic compounds associated with various printing operations, from letterpress to lithography to offset printing of either sheet-fed or continuous-fed presses in producing final printed copy. Lithography is the most common of the major printing processes (U.S. Environmental Protection Agency, 2007). Until 1995, up to 99 percent of the chemicals used in commercial printing were released to the air (U.S. Environmental Protection Agency, 1995), with the balance released to water or land or incorporated into the final printed product.

Volatile Organic Compounds

Offset printing is based on the repulsion between water and oil—the water-based processes use a fountain solution composed of water-soluble organic compounds such as alcohols and the oil-based processes include a plate cylinder to which ink is added (fig. 25; Kipphan, 2001). The plate can be made of zinc, aluminum, or lead, and often is created on-site with a linotype machine. The inked plate and the image to be printed never actually touch the paper to be printed but instead come into contact with the offset, or blanket, cylinder. Blanket cylinders typically are cleaned of old ink, paper fibers, and paper coatings before each press run or at the end of each shift to ensure excellent print quality (News&Tech, 2009).

One of the most commonly used solvents to clean blanket cylinders is called blanket wash (Sinha and Achenie, 2001). A 1992 survey of three commercial printers that used blanket-wash procedures indicated that blanket wash can consist of PCE, TCE, 1,1,1-trichloroethane (1,1,1-TCA), and toluene (Printers' National Environmental Assistance Center, 2011). The blanket wash is applied either manually or automatically, but has been primarily a manual process throughout the history of the commercial printing industry. The manual method, called "rag and bucket," involves wiping down the blanket cylinder with cloth rags dampened with blanket wash (Sinha and Achenie, 2001).

Prior to the establishment of industries in the 1970s to handle blanket-wash soiled rags, rag management was the responsibility of each pressroom. The amount of blanket wash solution used per pressroom is unknown, but has been estimated at 160 gallons per year (U.S. Environmental Protection Agency, 1997b). Blanket wash solutions typically are stored on site in 55–gallon drums. A list of the hazardous wastes commonly generated by the printing industry, called

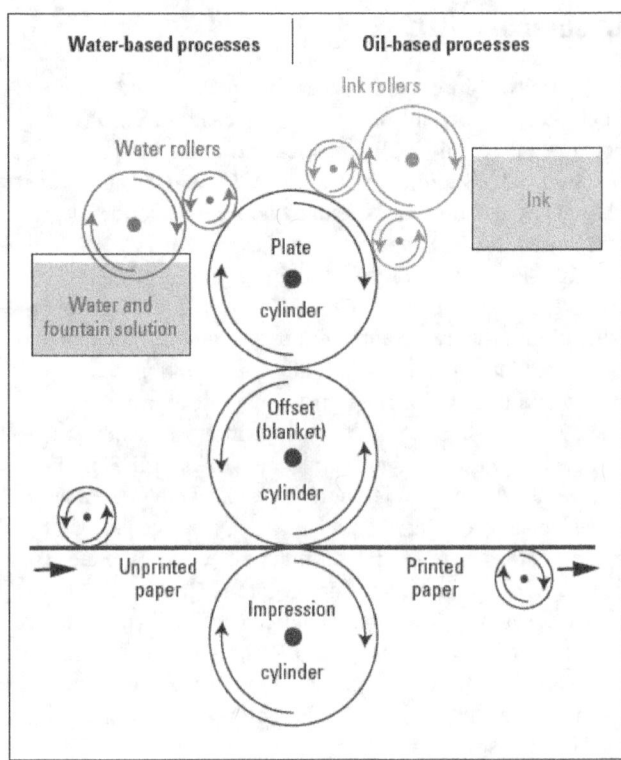

Figure Generalized diagram of the offset printing process in which blanket wash is used on the offset, or blanket, cylinder (modified from Kipphan, 2001).

the F-list or non-specific source wastes, is provided in table 9 (U.S. Environmental Protection Agency, 1997a). Included in the F-list are spent halogenated solvents used for degreasing and cleaning, including PCE, TCE, 1,1,1-TCA, CFC-113, methyl ethyl ketones, and non-halogenated solvents such as toluene.

In the 1960s, the commercial printing industry switched from alcohol-based blanket washes to those based on chlorinated solvents to decrease flammability risk and to accelerate drying times in the pressroom (table 1). Since about the 1990s, however, the commercial printing industry has switched from chlorinated solvents to vegetable-based solvents to meet more stringent requirements for VOC emissions to the atmosphere and to protect worker health.

Inorganic Compounds

Inorganic compounds also are used to meet a variety of needs in the commercial printing industry. Although some organic-based pigments have been used in inks, inorganic pigments composed of heavy metals have been used more often. Pigments (and corresponding inorganic elements) include white (titanium), yellow (bismuth, chromium, and cadmium), orange (molybdenum), blue (iron), green (chromium or copper), black (rubidium, strontium), and red (barium and zinc) (Buxbaum, 1998). Most pigments are composed of inorganic salts or oxides. Heavy metals, such as cobalt and

Table 9. Hazardous wastes on the F-list, including those used in the commercial printing industry (U.S. Environmental Protection Agency, 1997a).

[PCE, perchloroethylene; TCE, trichloroethylene; TCA, trichloroethane; CFC, chlorofluorocarbon]

Waste code	Waste (only chemicals used in highest volumes are listed)
F001	PCE
	TCE
	1,1,1-TCA
	CFC-113
F002	PCE
	TCE
	1,1,1-TCA
	CFC-113
F003	Xylene
	Toluene
	Methanol
F005	Toluene
	Methyl ethyl ketone
D005	Barium
D007	Chromium
D011	Silver

manganese also are used to facilitate drying of the printed material. Silver is used extensively by the commercial printing industry as a plate developer or photographic fixer (U.S. Environmental Protection Agency, 1997b). Acids, such as sulfuric acid, also are used (U.S. Environmental Protection Agency, 1997b, Appendix F). Moreover, organic-based fountain solutions also contain inorganic compounds, such as chromium, magnesium, phosphate, and silica. Mixtures of organic and inorganic compounds also are used in the commercial printing industry. For example, solvents are mixed with the pigments and dyes to act as the vehicle for inks, much like water is used with pigments to act as the vehicle for watercolor painting.

Commercial Printing in Montgomery

The commercial printing industry has been a part of the history of Montgomery, with a newspaper publishing and printing operation having occupied multiple locations in Montgomery since 1828 in addition to several smaller printing operations throughout the city (table 1; fig. 10). Responses to USEPA Section 104(e) Information Requests as part of the USEPA investigations on the CCP Site indicate that chemicals used during the commercial printing operations along Washington Avenue resulted in the generation of wastewater in the pre-press area. This wastewater was disposed of down floor drains or sinks that were connected either directly to the

sanitary sewer system or indirectly to the stormwater system. Soiled rags used with the blanket-wash process also were laundered on-site with discharge to a sump and then by pipe to Washington Avenue and into the stormwater system; such on-site laundering was a widespread practice until the late 1970s when soiled rags were laundered off-site by contractors (U.S. Environmental Protection Agency, 2009a). Moreover, soiled rags sometimes were disposed of down drains—rags were found in the sewer and stormwater pipes in downtown Montgomery by MWWSSB employees (Buddy Morgan, Montgomery Water Works and Sanitary Sewer Board, oral commun., November 16, 2009). Smaller, color-printing operations also were conducted at the southeastern intersection of Washington Avenue and McDonough Street using the same waste-disposal practices. At this location, responses to USEPA Section 104(e) Information Requests indicate that blanket washes were used on rags, spent fountain solutions were disposed of down a sink, and plate developers also were disposed of down the sink (U.S. Environmental Protection Agency, 2009a). It is unknown, however, what waste-disposal practices were used prior to the 1940s at the former locations of the newspaper publishing and printing operations at Dexter Avenue and Perry Street. Other smaller, separate printing operations located along Dexter Avenue near its intersection with Decatur Street also disposed of printing-related wastes into the sanitary sewer pipes, according to responses to USEPA Section 104(e) Information Requests (U.S. Environmental Protection Agency, 2009a). These waste-disposal activities primarily occurred prior to the enactment of the Resource Conservation and Recovery Act in 1976 and CERCLA in 1980 (table 1) legislation passed to address the increasing volume of municipal and industrial wastes in the United States.

Conclusions

The data collected between 2008 and 2010 by the USEPA and the USGS for additional assessments of the potential source area, contamination pathway, and the probable release history at the CCP Site support the following:

Potential Source Area:

1. The detection during August 2008 of TCE in core samples from trees growing along Washington Avenue indicates a near-surface residual source of TCE in that immediate area. The detection during April–May 2009 of TCE concentrations in groundwater from adjacent well MW-9S confirms the localized presence of TCE.

2. The presence, as early as 2000, of concentrations of VOCs greater than 10 ppm as measured using an FID in sediments cored from the 50-ft-thick unsaturated zone during vibracore drilling and installation of wells MW-9S and MW-10S confirm a near-surface residual source of VOC contamination in the vicinity of Washington and Dexter Avenues, respectively.

3. The detection during August 2008 of PCE in trees growing at the intersection of Perry Street with Dexter Avenue indicates a near-surface residual source of PCE in that immediate area. PCE also has been detected downgradient from these trees in groundwater samples collected from well MW-4S since 2000.

4. Future investigations at the CCP Site to supplement data presented in this report may reveal additional source areas related to the past disposal of wastes that contained chlorinated solvents.

Probable Contamination Pathway:

1. Concentrations of TCE were detected during August 2008 in core samples from trees growing along McDonough Street between a suspected potential source area of TCE along Washington Avenue and the detection of TCE concentrations in groundwater in downgradient well MW-1S. These trees are in general alignment with the sanitary sewer system beneath McDonough Street. Other information (responses to USEPA Section 104(e) Information Requests; high VOC concentrations in sediments cored from the unsaturated zone during installation of well MW-9S; and TCE concentrations detected in tree cores from T64 and T61 along Washington Avenue) indicates a probable source of TCE from the former commercial printing industry in that area.

2. Concentrations of PCE were detected in core samples from trees growing along Perry Street during August 2008. The trees are in general alignment with the sanitary sewer and stormwater systems beneath Washington Avenue and Perry Street. These tree-core detections indicate that wastewater that contained PCE entered and leaked from the sanitary sewer system and (or) was released to the stormwater system.

3. The absence of VOC concentrations in sediments cored from near land surface during the installation of well pairs MW-1S,I and MW-4S,I in 2000 and the presence of VOC detections in sediments cored from near the water table indicate that PCE and TCE concentrations detected in groundwater in these wells did not occur by downward vertical migration through the unsaturated zone. Rather, the groundwater contamination by PCE and TCE resulted from lateral groundwater flow from upgradient source areas.

4. The detection of chloroform in groundwater from well MW-1S during 2009 at concentrations indicative of treated municipal water indicates the following potential contaminant pathway: PCE- and TCE-contaminated wastewater related to printing operations was released to sinks, sumps, and floor drains in buildings along Washington and Dexter Avenues. This wastewater entered the sanitary sewer and (or) stormwater systems, entered the deeper subsurface through leaks and (or) joints, and was transported through the thick unsaturated zone downgradient to an area near the water table at well MW-1S and where workers were exposed to vapors in 1993. Moreover, this potential contamination pathway remains viable as indicated by detections of SF_6 and CFC concentrations found in groundwater.

Probable Release History:

1. The disposal of PCE- and TCE-contaminated wastewater generated as part of various commercial printing operations into the sanitary sewer and (or) stormwater systems at the CCP Site most likely occurred at least from the 1940s through the 1970s. This timeframe coincides with the widespread use of chlorinated solvents by printing operations.

Summary

Between 2008 and 2010, the U.S. Geological Survey Alabama and South Carolina Water Science Centers, in cooperation with the U.S. Environmental Protection Agency, Region 4, Superfund Division, Superfund Remedial Branch, Section C, conducted assessments at the Capital City Plume (CCP) Site in downtown Montgomery, Alabama. These assessments were done to investigate the potential source area, contamination pathway, and the probable release history of perchloroethylene (PCE) and trichloroethylene (TCE) detected in groundwater at the CCP Site since 1991. The assessments included the collection of (1) pore water in 2008 from the hyporheic zone of a creek using passive-diffusion bag samplers; (2) tissue samples in 2008 and 2009 from trees growing in areas in downtown Montgomery characterized by groundwater contamination and from trees growing in riparian zones along the Alabama River and Cypress Creek; and (3) groundwater samples in 2009 and 2010. The data collected indicate that the PCE- and TCE-contaminated shallow aquifer beneath the CCP Site most likely resulted from past use and disposal of industrial wastewater containing chlorinated solvents into the sanitary sewer and (or) stormwater systems by commercial printing industries that had occupied multiple locations in downtown Montgomery. Moreover, this scenario of chlorinated-solvent use and disposal occurred at least between the 1940s and 1970s at locations occupied by commercial printing operations. The data also indicate that a source of PCE and TCE contamination continues to exist in the shallow subsurface near the original release areas and that PCE and TCE have been transported to the intermediate part of the shallow aquifer.

References

Alabama Department of Public Health, 2004, Public Health Assessment Capital City Plume, Montgomery, Montgomery County, Alabama, CERCLIS No. AL0001058056, accessed October 1, 2008 at *http://www.atsdr.cdc.gov/HAC/pha/PHA. asp?docid=839&pg=0.*

Baes, C.F., and McLaughlin, S.B., 1984, Trace elements in tree rings—Evidence of recent and historical air pollution: Science, v. 224, no. 4648, p. 494–497.

Baes, C.F., and Ragsdale, H.L., 1981, Age-specific lead distribution in xylem rings of three tree genera in Atlanta, Georgia: Environmental Pollution (Series B, Chemical and Physical), v. 2, no. 1, p. 21–35.

Balouet, J.C., and Oudijk, G., 2006, The use of dendro-ecological methods to estimate the time frame of environmental releases: Environmental Claims Journal, v. 18, p. 1–18.

Balouet, J.C., Oudijk, G., Smith, K.T., Petrisor, I., Grudd, H., and Stocklassa, B., 2007, Applied dendroecology and environmental forensics. Characterizing and age dating environmental releases—Fundamentals and case studies: Environmental Forensics, v. 8, p. 1–17.

Balouet, J.C., Smith, K.T., Vroblesky, D., and Oudijk, G., 2009, Use of dendrochronology and dendrochemistry in environmental forensics—Does it meet the Daubert criteria?: Environmental Forensics, v. 10, no. 4, p. 268–276.

Black & Veatch, 2002, Remedial Investigation Report to the U.S. Environmental Protection Agency, Capital City Plume Site, Montgomery, Montgomery County, Alabama, various pagination, dated November 8, 2002.

Burken, J.G., Vroblesky, D.A., and Balouet, J.C., 2011, Phytoforensics, dendrochemistry, and phytoscreening—New green tools for delineating contaminants from past and present: Environmental Science & Technology, v. 45, no. 15, p. 6218–6226; accessible at *http://pubs.acs.org/doi/ pdf/10.1021/es2005286.*

Busenberg, Eurybiades, and Plummer, L.N., 1997, Use of sulfur hexafluoride as a dating tool and as a tracer of igneous and volcanic fluids in ground water [abs]: Geological Society of America, Salt Lake City, 1997, Abstracts with Programs, v. 29, no. 6, p. A–78.

Busenberg, Eurybiades, and Plummer, L.N., 2000, Dating young groundwater with sulfur hexafluoride—Natural and anthropogenic sources of sulfur hexafluoride: Water Resources Research, v. 36, no. 10, p. 3011–3030.

Buxbaum, G., ed., 1998, Industrial inorganic pigments: Wiley-VCH Verlag GmbH, Weinheim, 289 p.

Church, P.E., Vroblesky, D.A., and Lyford, F.P., 2002, Guidance on the use of passive-vapor-diffusion samplers to detect volatile organic compounds in ground-water discharge areas, and example applications in New England: U.S. Geological Survey Water-Resources Investigations Report 2002–4186, 79 p.

Elemental Analysis Incorporated, 2008, EAI PIXE laboratory quality assurance/quality control document. Various pagination.

Environmental Materials Consultants, Inc., 2003, Environmental site assessment, Montgomery Advertiser Properties, Montgomery, Alabama, 36104, prepared for The Montgomery County Commission, dated August 12, 2003, 22 p.

Ferguson, C.W., and Graybill, D.A., 1983, Dendrochronology of bristlecone pine—A progress report: Radiocarbon, v. 25, p. 287–288.

Hall, J.M., 2007, Ground water monitoring report, Capital City Plume Site, unpublished consultant report prepared for the City of Montgomery, August 2007, various pagination.

Hagemeyer, J., and Schäfer, H., 1995, Seasonal variations in concentrations and radial distribution patterns of Cd, Pb, and Zn in stem wood of beech trees (*Fagus sylvatica* L.): The Science of the Total Environment, v. 166, p. 77–87.

Hagemeyer, J., Schäfer, H., and Breckle, S.-W., 1994, Seasonal variations of nickel concentrations in annual xylem rings of beech trees (*Fagus sylvatica* L.): The Science of the Total Environment, v. 145, p. 111–118.

Ivahnenko, Tamara, and Barbash, J.E., 2004, Chloroform in the hydrologic system—Sources, transport, fate, occurrence, and effects on human health and aquatic organisms: U.S. Geological Survey Scientific Investigations Report 2004–5137, 34 p.

Ivahnenko, Tamara, and Zogorski, J.S., 2006, Sources and occurrence of chloroform and other trihalomethanes in drinking-water supply wells in the United States, 1986–2001: U.S. Geological Survey Scientific Investigations Report 2006–5015, 13 p.

Kipphan, H., 2001, Handbook of print media—Technologies and production methods: Springer, 1,207 p.

Knowles, D.B., Reade, H.L., Jr., and Scott, J.C., 1963, Geology and ground-water resources of Montgomery County, Alabama: U.S. Geological Survey Water-Supply Paper 1606, 73 p.

Landmeyer, J.E., 2001, Monitoring the effect of poplar trees on petroleum-hydrocarbon and chlorinated-solvent contaminated ground water: International Journal of Phytoremediation, v. 3, p. 61–85.

Landmeyer, J.E., Vroblesky, D.A., and Bradley, P.M., 2000, MTBE and BTEX in trees above gasoline-contaminated ground water: Case studies in the remediation of chlorinated and recalcitrant compounds, Wickramanayake, G.B., Gavaskar, A.R., Gibbs, J.T., and Means, J.L. (eds), Battelle Press, Columbus, OH, p. 17–24.

Lewis, T.E., 1995, Tree rings as indicators of ecosystem health: Boca Raton, FL, CRC Press, Inc., 210 p.

Malcolm Pirnie, Inc., 2003, Feasibility study, Capital City Plume Site, Montgomery, Alabama, unpublished consultant report prepared for the City of Montgomery, Montgomery, Alabama, submitted to the U.S. Environmental Protection Agency, Region 4, October 2003, various pagination.

Minear, R.A., and Amy, G.L., eds., 1996, Disinfection by-products in water treatment—The chemistry of their formation and control: Boca Raton, FL, CRC Press, Inc., 502 p.

Montgomery Water Works and Sanitary Sewer Board, 2010, Water Quality Report, accessed March 15, 2011, at *https://www.mwwssb.com/water-quality/CCR/ccrfile.cfm?ccr=2010*.

Muskat, B.T., and Neeley, M.A., 1985, The way it was, 1850–1930—Photographs of Montgomery and her central Alabama neighbors: Landmarks Foundation of Montgomery.

Nabais, C., Freitas, H., and Hagemeyer, J., 1999. Dendro-analysis—A tool for biomonitoring environmental pollution? The Science of the Total Environment, v. 232, p. 33–37.

News&Tech, 2009, Press maintenance can improve quality, reduce waste, accessed on January 27, 2009, at *http://www.newsandtecharchives.com/issues/1999/05-99/nt/05-99_pressmaint.htm*.

Phipps, R.L., 1985, Collecting, preparing, crossdating, and measuring tree increment cores: U.S. Geological Survey Water-Resources Investigations Report 85–4148, 48 p.

Plummer, L.N., and Friedman, L.C., 1999, Tracing and dating young ground water: U.S. Geological Survey Fact Sheet 134–99, 4 p.

Printers' National Environmental Assistance Center; 2011, What is PNEAC?, accessed February 18, 2011, at *http://www.pneac.org/whatis.cfm*.

Robinson, J.L., 2002, Ground-water quality beneath an urban residential and commercial area, Montgomery, Alabama, 1999–2000: U.S. Geological Survey Water-Resources Investigations Report 02–4052, 37 p.

Schumacher, J.G., Stuckhoff, G.C., and Burken, J.G., 2004, Assessment of subsurface chlorinated solvent contamination using tree cores at the Front Street Site and a former dry cleaning facility at the Riverfront Superfund Site, New Haven, Missouri, 1999–2003: U.S. Geological Survey Scientific Investigations Report 2004–5049, 35 p.

Scott, J.C., Cobb, R.H., and Castleberry, R.D., 1987, Geohydrology and susceptibility of major aquifers to surface contamination in Alabama; Area 8: U.S. Geological Survey Water-Resources Investigations Report 86–4360, 70 p.

Sinha, M., and Achenie, L.E.K., 2001, Systematic design of blanket wash solvents with recovery considerations: Advances in Environmental Research, v. 5, p. 239–249.

U.S. Environmental Protection Agency, 1994, Printing industry and use cluster profile, accessed August 22, 2011, at *http://www.epa.gov/dfe/pubs/printing/cluster/*.

U.S. Environmental Protection Agency, 1995, Sector Notebook Project, Printing and Publishing, EPA Office of Compliance Sector Notebook Project, profile of the printing and publishing industry: EPA/310-R-95-014.

U.S. Environmental Protection Agency, 1997a, Design for the Environment Program, cleaner technologies substitute assessment—Lithographic blanket washes: EPA 744-R-97-006, accessed February 18, 2011, at *http://www.pneac.org/sheets/litho/litho.pdf*.

U.S. Environmental Protection Agency, 1997b, Blanket wash solutions for small printers: EPA7-F-95-005.

U.S. Environmental Protection Agency, 2000a, NPL Site narrative for Capital City Plume, accessed on October 1, 2008, at *http://www.epa.gov/superfund/sites/npl/nar1593.htm*.

U.S. Environmental Protection Agency, 2007, Pollution prevention in a lithographic pressroom, accessed April 16, 2009, at *www.epa.gov/region7/p2/lyle.htm*.

U.S. Environmental Protection Agency, 2009a, Capital City Plume Site Information Requests, Responses for 200 Washington Avenue, 116 McDonough Street, and 500 Dexter Avenue, Montgomery, Alabama, 104(e) Information Requests: various pagination.

U.S. Environmental Protection Agency, 2009b, Drinking water contaminants—National Primary Drinking Water Standards, accessed March 3, 2011, at *http://water.epa.gov/drink/contaminants/index.cfm*.

U.S. Geological Survey, variously dated, National field manual for the collection of water-quality data: U.S. Geological Survey Techniques of Water-Resources Investigations, book, 9, chap. A1, January, accessed July 12, 2009, at *http://pubs.water.usgs.gov/twri9A2/*.

Vroblesky, D.A., 2008, User's guide to the collection and analysis of tree cores to assess the distribution of subsurface volatile organic compounds: U.S. Geological Survey Scientific Investigations Report 2008–5088, 59 p.

Vroblesky, D.A., Canova, J.L., Bradley, P.M., and Landmeyer, J.E., 2009, Tritium concentrations in environmental samples and transpiration rates from the vicinity of Mary's Branch Creek and background areas, Barnwell, South Carolina, 2007–2009: U.S. Geological Survey Scientific Investigations Report, 2009–5245, 12 p.

Vroblesky, D.A., Clinton, B.D., Vose, J.M., Casey, C.C., Harvey, G.J., and Bradley, P.M., 2004, Ground water chlorinated ethenes in tree trunks—Case studies, influence of recharge, and potential degradation mechanisms: Ground Water Monitoring & Remediation, v. 24, no. 3, p. 124–138.

Vroblesky, D.A., Nietch, C.T., and Morris, J.T., 1999, Chlorinated ethenes from groundwater in tree trunks: Environmental Science & Technology, v. 33, p. 510–515.

Vroblesky, D.A., Petkewich, M.D., Landmeyer, J.E., and Lowery, M.A., 2009, Source, transport, and fate of groundwater contamination at Site 45, Marine Corps Recruit Depot, Parris Island, South Carolina: U.S. Geological Survey Scientific Investigations Report 2009–5161, 80 p.

Vroblesky, D.A., and Yanosky, T.M., 1990, Use of tree-ring chemistry to document historical ground-water contamination events: Ground Water, v. 28, p. 677–684.

Yanosky, T.M., Hansen, B.P., and Schening, M.R., 2001, Use of tree rings to investigate the onset of contamination of a shallow aquifer by chlorinated solvents: Journal of Contaminant Hydrology, v. 50, p. 159–173.

Zogorski, J.S., Carter, J.M., Ivahnenko, T., Lapham, W.W., Moran, M.J., Rowe, B.L., Squillace, P.J., and Toccalino, P.L., 2006, Volatile organic compounds in the Nation's ground water and drinking-water supply wells: U.S. Geological Survey Circular 1292, 101 p.

Table 2. Perchloroethylene, trichloroethylene, *cis*-1,2-dichloroethylene, benzene, and toluene concentrations in the headspace of vials that contained tree cores, Capital City Plume Site, Montgomery, Alabama, August 2008.

[ID, identification; Core ID, the unique position of a core or multiple cores collected from a particular tree; ppbv, parts per billion by volume of vial headspace; <, less than; μL, microliter; nm, not measured; ?, unknown]

Tree ID (figs. 9, 10)	Tree description	Core ID	Diameter at breast height (inches)	Core collection date	Core analysis date	Per-chloro-ethylene	Tri-chloro-ethylene	*cis*-1,2-dichloro-ethylene	Benzene and toluene	Heating time (seconds)	Comments and (or) volume of headspace sample injected into gas chromatograph
						Method reporting levels					
						2 ppbv	20 ppbv	15 ppbv	10 ppbv		
T1	Cottonwood	B		August 18, 2008	August 19, 2008	<2	<20	<15	<10	30	250 μL
T1		C		August 18, 2008	August 19, 2008	<2	<20	<15	<10	30	250 μL
T2	Sycamore	A	24	August 18, 2008	August 19, 2008	553	<20	<15	<10	30	250 μL
T2		B		August 18, 2008	August 19, 2008	511	61	<15	<10	30	250 μL
T2		C		August 18, 2008	August 19, 2008	167	31	<15	<10	30	250 μL
T2		AAA		August 19, 2008	August 19, 2008	39.75	<20	<15	<10	15	200 μL
T3	Sycamore	A	nm	August 18, 2008	August 19, 2008	<2	<20	<15	<10	30	250 μL
T3		B		August 18, 2008	August 19, 2008	<2	<20	<15	<10	30	250 μL
T3		C		August 18, 2008	August 19, 2008	<2	<20	<15	<10	30	250 μL
T3		D		August 18, 2008	August 19, 2008	<2	24	<15	<10	30	250 μL
T4	Sycamore	B	14	August 18, 2008	August 19, 2008	<2	<20	<15	<10	30	250 μL
T4		A		August 18, 2008	August 19, 2008	<2	<20	<15	<10	30	250 μL
T5	Cottonwood	B	31	August 18, 2008	August 19, 2008	<2	<20	<15	<10	30	250 μL
T5		C		August 18, 2008	August 19, 2008	<2	<20	<15	<10	30	250 μL
T5		Metals		August 19, 2008	August 21, 2008	120.6	37	<15	<10	8	Short microwave time; 200 μL.
T6	Catalpa	AA	17	August 19, 2008	August 19, 2008	<2	453	298	<10	30	Composite sample. 100 μL.
T7	Red maple	A	12	August 19, 2008	August 19, 2008	<2	<20	<15	<10	30	250 μL
T7		AR1		August 19, 2008	August 19, 2008	<2	68.23	<15	<10	30	Rerun of T7 A. 100 μL.
T7		AR2		August 19, 2008	August 19, 2008	<2	73.98	<15	<10	30	Composite sample. 250 μL. Rerun of T7 A.
T7		B		August 19, 2008	August 22, 2008	<2	<20	<15	<10	8	200 μL

Table 2.   Perchloroethylene, trichloroethylene, *cis*-1,2-dichloroethylene, benzene, and toluene concentrations in the headspace of vials that contained tree cores, Capital City Plume Site, Montgomery, Alabama, August 2008.—Continued

[ID, identification; Core ID, the unique position of a core or multiple cores collected from a particular tree; ppbv, parts per billion by volume of vial headspace; <, less than; µL, microliter; nm, not measured; ?, unknown]

Tree ID (figs. 9, 10)	Tree description	Core ID	Diameter at breast height (inches)	Core collection date	Core analysis date	Per-chloro-ethylene	Tri-chloro-ethylene	*cis*-1,2-dichloro-ethylene	Benzene and toluene	Heating time (seconds)	Comments and (or) volume of headspace sample injected into gas chromatograph
						2 ppbv	20 ppbv	15 ppbv	10 ppbv		
T8	Sycamore	A	12	August 19, 2008	August 19, 2008	<2	243	<15	<10	30	Composite sample. 100 µL.
T9	Cottonwood	A	31	August 19, 2008	August 19, 2008	<2	<20	<15	<10	15	Composite sample. 100 µL.
T10	China berry	SX2	32	August 19, 2008	August 19, 2008	<2	<20	<15	<10	15	Composite sample. 100 µL.
T10		SX2 rerun		August 19, 2008	August 19, 2008	<2	<20	<15	<10	20	Composite sample. 100 µL.
T10		B		August 19, 2008	August 19, 2008	<2	<20	<15	<10	15	Composite sample. 100 µL.
T11	Elm	Flower	nm	August 19, 2008	August 19, 2008	<2	<20	<15	<10	15	Flower sample. 100 µL.
T11				August 19, 2008	August 19, 2008	<2	<20	<15	<10	15	Composite sample. 100 µL.
T12	Catalpa	A	30	August 19, 2008	August 19, 2008	<2	<20	<15	<10	15	100 µL
T12		B1		August 19, 2008	August 19, 2008	14	168	<15	<10	30	250 µL
T12		B2		August 19, 2008	August 19, 2008	<2	<20	<15	<10	30	Reinjection of T12 B1.
T12		B3		August 19, 2008	August 19, 2008	<2	<20	<15	<10	30	Reinjection of T12 B1.
T12		B4		August 19, 2008	August 19, 2008	26	140	<15	<10	20	Reinjection of T12 B1.
T12		A2		August 19, 2008	August 19, 2008	<2	<20	<15	<10	20	Reinjection of T12 A; 250 µL.
T12		BD		August 19, 2008	August 20, 2008	<2	<100	<15	<10	8	Collected fresh cores from T12. Short micro-wave time; 200 µL.
T12		Cat1		August 19, 2008	August 19, 2008	<2	2,877	<15	<10	20	200 µL
T12		CATB		August 19, 2008	August 20, 2008	<2	<100	<15	<10	No heat.	200 µL
T12		CATC		August 19, 2008	August 20, 2008	<2	<100	<15	<10	8	Short heat; 200 µL.
T13	Pecan		nm	August 19, 2008	August 19, 2008	<2	<20	<15	<10	15	Composite sample. 200 µL.
T14	Willow		nm	August 19, 2008	August 19, 2008	<2	61	<15	<10	15	Composite sample. 200 µL.

Table 2   47

Table 2. Perchloroethylene, trichloroethylene, *cis*-1,2-dichloroethylene, benzene, and toluene concentrations in the headspace of vials that contained tree cores, Capital City Plume Site, Montgomery, Alabama, August 2008.—Continued

[ID, identification; Core ID, the unique position of a core or multiple cores collected from a particular tree; ppbv, parts per billion by volume of vial headspace; <, less than; µL, microliter; nm, not measured; ?, unknown]

Tree ID (figs. 9, 10)	Tree description	Core ID	Diameter at breast height (inches)	Core collection date	Core analysis date	Per-chloro-ethylene	Tri-chloro-ethylene	*cis*-1,2-dichloro-ethylene	Benzene and toluene	Heating time (seconds)	Comments and (or) volume of headspace sample injected into gas chromatograph
						2 ppbv	20 ppbv	15 ppbv	10 ppbv		
T15	Oak		44	August 19, 2008	August 19, 2008	<2	<20	<15	<10	15	Composite sample. 200 µL.
T16	Sycamore		14	August 19, 2008	August 19, 2008	<2	<20	<15	<10	15	Composite sample. 200 µL.
T17	Gingko		13	August 19, 2008	August 19, 2008	<2	254	<15	<10	15	Composite sample. 200 µL.
T18	Oak		nm	August 19, 2008	August 19, 2008	<2	302	<15	<10	15	Composite sample. 200 µL.
T19	Oak	A	21	August 19, 2008	August 19, 2008	<2	104.8	<15	<10	15	Composite sample. 200 µL.
T19		B		August 19, 2008	August 19, 2008	<2	<20	<15	<10	15	Composite sample. 200 µL.
T20	Gingko	A	19	August 19, 2008	August 19, 2008	<2	<20	<15	<10	15	200 µL
T20		B		August 19, 2008	August 20, 2008	<2	<20	<15	<10	8	Short microwave time; 200 µL.
T21	Oak	A	17	August 19, 2008	August 19, 2008	<2	38	<15	<10	15	200 µL
T21	Oak	A		August 19, 2008	August 19, 2008	<2	70	<15	<10	15	200 µL
T21		B		August 19, 2008	August 19, 2008	<2	84	<15	<10	15	200 µL
T22	Sycamore	A	17	August 19, 2008	August 19, 2008	<2	<20	<15	<10	15	Injected 200 µL.
T22		B		August 19, 2008	August 19, 2008	<2	32	<15	<10	15	Injected 200 µL.
T23	Maple	A	7	August 19, 2008	August 19, 2008	<2	<20	<15	<10	12	Injected 200 µL.
T23		B		August 19, 2008	August 19, 2008	<2	<20	<15	<10	14	Injected 200 µL.
T24	Oak	A	32	August 19, 2008	August 20, 2008	<2	<100	<15	<10	8	Short microwave time because tree core was collected 8/19; Injected 200 µL.
T24		B		August 19, 2008	August 20, 2008	<2	<100	<15	<10	8	Short microwave time because tree core was collected 8/19; Injected 200 µL.

Table 2.   Perchloroethylene, trichloroethylene, *cis*-1,2-dichloroethylene, benzene, and toluene concentrations in the headspace of vials that contained tree cores, Capital City Plume Site, Montgomery, Alabama, August 2008.—Continued

[ID, identification; Core ID, the unique position of a core or multiple cores collected from a particular tree; ppbv, parts per billion by volume of vial headspace; <, less than; µL, microliter; nm, not measured; ?, unknown]

Tree ID (figs. 9, 10)	Tree description	Core ID	Diameter at breast height (inches)	Core collection date	Core analysis date	Per-chloro-ethylene	Tri-chloro-ethylene	*cis*-1,2-dichloro-ethylene	Benzene and toluene	Heating time (seconds)	Comments and (or) volume of headspace sample injected into gas chromatograph
						Method reporting levels					
						2 ppbv	20 ppbv	15 ppbv	10 ppbv		
T25	Magnolia	A	13	August 19, 2008	August 20, 2008	<2	<100	<15	<10	8	Short microwave time because tree core was collected 8/19; Injected 200 µL.
T25		B		August 19, 2008	August 20, 2008	<2	<100	<15	<10	8	Short microwave time because tree core was collected 8/19; Injected 200 µL.
T26	Gingko	A	9.75	August 19, 2008	August 20, 2008	<2	<100	<15	<10	8	Short microwave time because tree core was collected 8/19; Injected 200 µL.
T26		B		August 19, 2008	August 20, 2008	<2	<100	<15	<10	8	Short microwave time because tree core was collected 8/19; Injected 200 µL.
T27	Oak	A	12	August 19, 2008	August 20, 2008	<2	<100	<15	<10	8	Short microwave time because tree core was collected 8/19; Injected 200 µL.
T27		B		August 19, 2008	August 20, 2008	<2	<100	<15	<10	8	Short microwave time because tree core was collected 8/19; Injected 200 µL.
T28	Oak	A	14	August 19, 2008	August 20, 2008	<2	<100	<15	<10	8	Short microwave time because tree core was collected 8/19; Injected 200 µL.
T28		B		August 19, 2008	August 20, 2008	<2	92	<15	<10	8	Short microwave time because tree core was collected 8/19; Injected 200 µL.

Table 2   49

Table 2. Perchloroethylene, trichloroethylene, *cis*-1,2-dichloroethylene, benzene, and toluene concentrations in the headspace of vials that contained tree cores, Capital City Plume Site, Montgomery, Alabama, August 2008.—Continued

[ID, identification; Core ID, the unique position of a core or multiple cores collected from a particular tree; ppbv, parts per billion by volume of vial headspace; <, less than; μL, microliter; nm, not measured; ?, unknown]

Tree ID (figs. 9, 10)	Tree description	Core ID	Diameter at breast height (inches)	Core collection date	Core analysis date	Per-chloro-ethylene	Tri-chloro-ethylene	*cis*-1,2-dichloro-ethylene	Benzene and toluene	Heating time (seconds)	Comments and (or) volume of headspace sample injected into gas chromatograph
						2 ppbv	20 ppbv	15 ppbv	10 ppbv		
T29	Oak	A	8	August 19, 2008	August 20, 2008	<2	144	<15	<10	8	Short microwave time because tree core was collected 8/19; Injected 200 μL.
T29		B		August 19, 2008	August 20, 2008	<2	301	<15	<10	8	Short microwave time because tree core was collected 8/19; Injected 200 μL.
T30	Oak	A	10	August 19, 2008	August 20, 2008	<2	<20	<15	<10	8	Short microwave time because tree core was collected 8/19; Injected 200 μL.
T30		B		August 19, 2008	August 20, 2008	<2	<20	<15	<10	8	Short microwave time because tree core was collected 8/19; Injected 200 μL.
T31	Oak	A	26	August 20, 2008	August 20, 2008	<2	693	<15	<10	12	Injected 200 μL.
T31		A		August 20, 2008	August 20, 2008	<2	307	<15	<10		Injected 200 μL.
T31		B1		August 20, 2008	August 20, 2008	29	142	<15	<10	12	Injected 200 μL.
T31		B2		August 20, 2008	August 20, 2008	42	175	<15	<10	Reheated 12 sec	Injected 200 μL.
T32	Oak	A	14	August 20, 2008	August 20, 2008	5,082	401	<15	<10	12	Injected 200 μL.
T32		B		August 20, 2008	August 22, 2008	8,782	<20	<15	<10	8	Injected 200 μL.
T33	Oak	A	11	August 20, 2008	August 20, 2008	<2	<20	<15	<10	12	Injected 200 μL.
T33		B		August 20, 2008	August 20, 2008	<2	257	<15	<10	12	Injected 200 μL.
T34	Oak	A	11	August 20, 2008	August 20, 2008	<2	<20	<15	<10	12	Injected 200 μL.
T34		B		August 20, 2008	August 20, 2008	<2	<20	<15	<10	12	Injected 200 μL.

Table 2. Perchloroethylene, trichloroethylene, *cis*-1,2-dichloroethylene, benzene, and toluene concentrations in the headspace of vials that contained tree cores, Capital City Plume Site, Montgomery, Alabama, August 2008.—Continued

[ID, identification; Core ID, the unique position of a core or multiple cores collected from a particular tree; ppbv, parts per billion by volume of vial headspace; <, less than; μL, microliter; nm, not measured; ?, unknown]

Tree ID (figs. 9, 10)	Tree description	Core ID	Diameter at breast height (inches)	Core collection date	Core analysis date	Per-chloro-ethylene	Tri-chloro-ethylene	*cis*-1,2-dichloro-ethylene	Benzene and toluene	Heating time (seconds)	Comments and (or) volume of headspace sample injected into gas chromatograph
							Method reporting levels				
						2 ppbv	20 ppbv	15 ppbv	10 ppbv		
T35	Oak	A	12	August 20, 2008	August 20, 2008	<2	<20	<15	<10	12	Injected 200 μL.
T35		B		August 20, 2008	August 20, 2008	<2	136	<15	<10	12	Injected 200 μL.
T36	?	A	24	August 20, 2008	August 20, 2008	<2	<20	<15	<10	12	Injected 200 μL.
T36		B		August 20, 2008	August 20, 2008	<2	<20	<15	<10	12	Injected 200 μL.
T37	?	A	17	August 20, 2008	August 20, 2008	<2	<20	<15	<10	12	Injected 200 μL.
T37		B		August 20, 2008	August 20, 2008	<2	<20	<15	<10	12	Injected 200 μL.
T38	Gingko	A	16	August 20, 2008	August 20, 2008	44	<20	<15	<10	12	Injected 200 μL.
T38		B		August 20, 2008	August 20, 2008	trace(26)	<20	<15	<10	12	Injected 200 μL.
T39	Gingko	A	13	August 20, 2008	August 20, 2008	66	<20	<15	<10	12	Injected 200 μL.
T39		B		August 20, 2008	August 20, 2008	29	<20	<15	<10	12	Injected 200 μL.
T39		C(fruit)		August 20, 2008	August 20, 2008	<2	<20	<15	<10	12	Injected 200 μL.
T40	Oak	A	22	August 20, 2008	August 20, 2008	<2	<20	<15	<10	12	Injected 200 μL.
T40		B		August 20, 2008	August 20, 2008	<2	<20	<15	<10	12	Injected 200 μL.
T41	Oak	A	14	August 20, 2008	August 20, 2008	<2	142	<15	<10	12	Injected 200 μL.
T41		B		August 20, 2008	August 20, 2008	<2	<20	<15	<10	12	Injected 200 μL.
T41		C		August 20, 2008	August 20, 2008	<2	<20	<15	<10	12	Injected 200 μL.
T42	Oak	A	13	August 20, 2008	August 20, 2008	<2	<20	<15	<10	12	Injected 200 μL.
T43	Oak	A	14	August 20, 2008	August 20, 2008	<2	<20	<15	<10	12	Injected 200 μL.
T43		B		August 20, 2008	August 20, 2008	<2	102	<15	<10	12	Injected 200 μL.

Table 2   51

Table 2.   Perchloroethylene, trichloroethylene, *cis*-1,2-dichloroethylene, benzene, and toluene concentrations in the headspace of vials that contained tree cores, Capital City Plume Site, Montgomery, Alabama, August 2008.—Continued

[ID, identification; Core ID, the unique position of a core or multiple cores collected from a particular tree; ppbv, parts per billion by volume of vial headspace; <, less than; μL, microliter; nm, not measured; ?, unknown]

Tree ID (figs. 9, 10)	Tree description	Core ID	Diameter at breast height (inches)	Core collection date	Core analysis date	Per-chloro-ethylene	Tri-chloro-ethylene	*cis*-1,2-dichloro-ethylene	Benzene and toluene	Heating time (seconds)	Comments and (or) volume of headspace sample injected into gas chromatograph
						Method reporting levels					
						2 ppbv	20 ppbv	15 ppbv	10 ppbv		
T44	Oak	A	19	August 20, 2008	August 20, 2008	<2	<20	<15	<10	12	Injected 200 μL.
T44		B		August 20, 2008	August 20, 2008	<2	<20	<15	<10	12	Injected 200 μL.
T45	Oak	A	14	August 20, 2008	August 20, 2008	<2	<20	<15	<10	12	Injected 200 μL.
T45		B		August 20, 2008	August 20, 2008	<2	<20	<15	<10	12	Injected 200 μL.
T46	Oak	A	14	August 20, 2008	August 20, 2008	<2	<20	<15	<10	12	Injected 200 μL.
T46		B		August 20, 2008	August 20, 2008	<2	<20	<15	<10	12	Injected 200 μL.
T47	Oak	A	20	August 20, 2008	August 20, 2008	<2	524	<15	<10	12	Injected 200 μL.
T47		B		August 20, 2008	August 20, 2008	<2	891	<15	<10	12	Injected 200 μL.
T48	Pear	A	13	August 20, 2008	August 22, 2008	<2	<20	<15	<10	8	Injected 200 μL.
T49	Elm	B	12	August 20, 2008	August 22, 2008	<2	<20	<15	<10	8	Injected 200 μL.
T49		A		August 20, 2008	August 22, 2008	<2	<20	<15	<10	8	Injected 200 μL.
T50	Oak	A	13.5	August 20, 2008	August 22, 2008	<2	<20	<15	<10	8	Injected 200 μL.
T50		B		August 20, 2008	August 22, 2008	<2	<20	<15	<10	8	Injected 200 μL.
T51	Oak	A	12	August 20, 2008	August 21, 2008	<2	<20	<15	<10	16	Injected 200 μL.
T51		B		August 20, 2008	August 21, 2008	<2	<20	<15	<10	8	Injected 200 μL.
T52	Elm	A	38	August 20, 2008	August 21, 2008	<2	<20	<15	<10	8	Slight TCE peak-wave.
T52		B		August 20, 2008	August 21, 2008	<2	<20	<15	<10	8	Injected 200 μL.
T53	Maple	B1	10	August 20, 2008	August 22, 2008	<2	<20	<15	Large late peak	8	Injected 200 μL.
T53		B2		August 20, 2008	August 22, 2008	<2	<20	<15	Large late peak	8	Injected 200 μL.

Table 2.   Perchloroethylene, trichloroethylene, *cis*-1,2-dichloroethylene, benzene, and toluene concentrations in the headspace of vials that contained tree cores, Capital City Plume Site, Montgomery, Alabama, August 2008.—Continued

[ID, identification; Core ID, the unique position of a core or multiple cores collected from a particular tree; ppbv, parts per billion by volume of vial headspace; <, less than; µL, microliter; nm, not measured; ?, unknown]

Tree ID (figs. 9, 10)	Tree description	Core ID	Diameter at breast height (inches)	Core collection date	Core analysis date	Per-chloro-ethylene	Tri-chloro-ethylene	*cis*-1,2-dichloro-ethylene	Benzene and toluene	Heating time (seconds)	Comments and (or) volume of headspace sample injected into gas chromatograph
						Method reporting levels					
						2 ppbv	20 ppbv	15 ppbv	10 ppbv		
T53A			10	August 20, 2008	August 21, 2008	<2	<20	<15	<10	8	Short microwave time because tree core was collected 8/20; Injected 200 µL.
T54	Pine	A	28	August 20, 2008	August 21, 2008	<2	<20	<15	<10		Injected 200 µL.
T54		AR		August 20, 2008	August 21, 2008	<2	<20	<15	<10		
T54		AR2		August 20, 2008	August 22, 2008	<2	<20	<15	Toluene (103)	8	Injected 200 µL.
T54		B		August 20, 2008	August 22, 2008	<2	<20	<15	Toluene (95)	8	Injected 200 µL.
T55	Ginkgo	A	14	August 20, 2008	August 20, 2008	<2	<20	<15	<10	12	Injected 200 µL.
T55		B		August 20, 2008	August 20, 2008	<2	<20	<15	<10	12	Injected 200 µL.
T56	Ginkgo	A		August 20, 2008	August 20, 2008	<2	<20	<15	<10	12	Injected 200 µL.
T56		B		August 20, 2008	August 20, 2008	<2	<20	<15	<10	12	Injected 200 µL.
T57	Ginkgo	A	13	August 20, 2008	August 20, 2008	<2	<20	<15	<10	12	Injected 200 µL.
T57		B		August 20, 2008	August 20, 2008	<2	<20	<15	<10	12	Injected 200 µL.
T58	Ginkgo	A	20	August 20, 2008	August 20, 2008	<2	<20	<15	<10	12	Injected 200 µL.
T58		B		August 20, 2008	August 20, 2008	<2	<20	<15	<10	12	Injected 200 µL.
T59	Oak	A	22	August 20, 2008	August 20, 2008	<2	<20	<15	<10	12	Injected 200 µL.
T59		B		August 20, 2008	August 20, 2008	<2	<20	<15	<10	12	Injected 200 µL.
T60	Oak	A	13	August 20, 2008	August 20, 2008	<2	<20	<15	<10	12	Injected 200 µL.
T60		B		August 20, 2008	August 20, 2008	<2	<20	<15	<10	12	Injected 200 µL.
T61	Oak	A	25	August 20, 2008	August 20, 2008	<2	176	<15	<10	12	Injected 200 µL.
T61		B		August 20, 2008	August 20, 2008	<2	<20	<15	<10	12	Injected 200 µL.

Table 2   53

Table 2. Perchloroethylene, trichloroethylene, *cis*-1,2-dichloroethylene, benzene, and toluene concentrations in the headspace of vials that contained tree cores, Capital City Plume Site, Montgomery, Alabama, August 2008.—Continued

[ID, identification; Core ID, the unique position of a core or multiple cores collected from a particular tree; ppbv, parts per billion by volume of vial headspace; <, less than; μL, microliter; nm, not measured; ?, unknown]

Tree ID (figs. 9, 10)	Tree description	Core ID	Diameter at breast height (inches)	Core collection date	Core analysis date	Per-chloro-ethylene	Tri-chloro-ethylene	*cis*-1,2-dichloro-ethylene	Benzene and toluene	Heating time (seconds)	Comments and (or) volume of headspace sample injected into gas chromatograph
						2 ppbv	20 ppbv	15 ppbv	10 ppbv		
T62	Oak	A	23	August 20, 2008	August 20, 2008	<2	<20	<15	<10	12	Injected 200 μL.
T62		B		August 20, 2008	August 20, 2008	<2	<20	<15	<10	12	Injected 200 μL.
T63	Oak	A	18	August 20, 2008	August 20, 2008	<2	<20	<15	<10	12	Injected 200 μL.
T63		B		August 20, 2008	August 20, 2008	<2	<20	<15	<10	12	Injected 200 μL.
T64	Oak	A	28	August 20, 2008	August 20, 2008	<2	68,650	573	<10	12	Injected 200 μL.
T64		B		August 20, 2008	August 22, 2008	<2	4,657	30	<10	8	Injected 200 μL.
T65	Oak	A	12.5	August 20, 2008	August 20, 2008	<2	<20	<15	<10	12	Injected 200 μL.
T65		B		August 20, 2008	August 20, 2008	<2	<20	<15	<10	12	Injected 200 μL.
T66	Oak	A	11.5	August 20, 2008	August 20, 2008	<2	<20	<15	<10	12	Injected 200 μL.
T66		B		August 20, 2008	August 20, 2008	<2	<20	<15	<10	12	Injected 200 μL.
T67	Oak	B	13	August 20, 2008	August 20, 2008	<2	<20	<15	<10	12	Injected 200 μL.
T67		A		August 20, 2008	August 20, 2008	<2	<20	<15	<10	12	Injected 200 μL.
T68	Oak	A	8	August 20, 2008	August 20, 2008	<2	<20	<15	<10	12	Injected 200 μL.
T68		B		August 20, 2008	August 20, 2008	<2	<20	<15	<10	12	Injected 200 μL.
T69	Oak	C	6	August 20, 2008	August 20, 2008	<2	<20	<15	<10	12	Injected 200 μL.
T69		A		August 20, 2008	August 20, 2008	<2	<20	<15	<10	12	Injected 200 μL.
T69		B		August 20, 2008	August 20, 2008	<2	<20	<15	<10	12	Injected 200 μL.
Air				August 20, 2008	August 20, 2008	<2	<20	<15	<10	8	Injected 200 μL.
				August 22, 2008	August 22, 2008	<2	<20	<15	<10	8	Injected 200 μL.